EM

BOOKS

Making Music With Your Computer

From the editors of *Electronic Musician* magazine

■ ■ ■

Edited by David (Rudy) Trubitt

HLP *Hal Leonard Publishing Corporation*

1993 EMBooks

Printed in Winona, Minnesota, USA

Library of Congress Catalog Card Number: 92-075170

These articles were previously published in a somewhat different form in *Electronic Musician* magazine.

Production staff: Brad Smith, general manager; Peter Hirschfeld, series director; Bob O'Donnell, editorial director; Ellen Richman, production director; Andy Jewett and Mary Cosola, editorial assistants.
Design staff: Gelfand Graphic Design. Barbara Gelfand, art director; Emma Rybakova, production artist.
Special thanks to the staff and freelance writers of *Electronic Musician*.

EMBooks
6400 Hollis St., Suite 12
Emeryville, CA 94608
(510) 653-3307

Also from EMBooks:
Electronic Musician's Tech Terms

Also from MixBooks:
Concert Sound
Sound For Picture
Music Producers
Hal Blaine and the Wrecking Crew
Studio Life
Auditory Perception Course

EMBooks and MixBooks are divisions of Act III Publishing.

ISBN 0-7935-1990-X

Table of Contents

Introduction

If you've heard about making music with computers and want to learn more, this book is for you. Whether you're a computer user trying to come to grips with electronic music technology or a musician searching for the right computer, **Making Music With Your Computer** will help you get started. This collection of articles from *Electronic Musician* magazine will guide you through all major aspects of computer music. It begins with a broad overview and then leaves you free to explore the topics you're most interested in.

First, we'll look at the many ways computers can contribute to the music-making process. Then we'll take a look at the bridge that made the computer/music union possible—the Musical Instrument Digital Interface, or MIDI. The next step will be de-mystifying the many concepts and buzzwords surrounding electronic music technology. Then, we'll talk about choosing the right computer and MIDI equipment for your needs.

Of course, all that will be just a prelude to the main event—making music. We'll cover the most popular types of music software, including programs for recording your music and printing it out for others to play.

Multimedia and digital sound is another exciting topic, so we've included articles that explain how computers can record and manipulate digital audio, using the same type of technology that brought us the compact disc. We'll also cover one of the industry's biggest buzzwords, *multimedia*, and explain its link to music and sound.

Finally, our appendix has a list of musical instrument and software companies, along with advice on the most effective ways to get help from software developers if you get stuck. The appendix also includes an extensive glossary of terms and a comprehensive index to help you find the information you need quickly.

With your enthusiasm and persistence, this book will be the guide that brings you into the world of computers and electronic music. Happy travels!

BY DAVID (RUDY) TRUBITT

Foreword

Technology and music have always been partners. The musician is limited only by his or her imagination and the capabilities of available instruments. As such, since early civilization, people have been using the latest technology in their quest to create new instruments to better release the music in their heads.

Hollowed logs with animal skins became drums, while reeds and bamboo became melody instruments. As woodworking skills were developed, lutes and other stringed instruments evolved. With the discovery of metal-making and brass, a whole new genre of musical instruments was created. As new materials were developed, musical instruments continued to be transformed and invented. New technology in the 1700's allowed the harpsichord to gain expressiveness by playing soft and loud, becoming the pianoforte, more commonly known as the piano.

The harnessing of electricity provided another opportunity for creating new instruments. After some marginally successful attempts at incorporating electricity for use in music-making, such as the Theremin, electric guitars and organs became the first popular conduits for this new technology. Soon the transistor was recruited for music duty and the synthesizer was born.

The next milestone in applicable technology was the microprocessor. This spawned the microcomputer and another new generation of musical instruments. Most importantly, the microprocessor allowed the microcomputer and these new instruments to work together, creating a whole new set of capabilities.

With these new adaptations of technology to music-making came new styles of music. Since the timbre, or sound, of an instrument is created by the unique combination of overtones indigenous to each instrument, musicians tended to "hear" music that was in harmony with the specific overtones of each instrument. When a new instrument was developed, a new palette of overtones was created which inspired new music.

BY PETER HIRSCHFELD

Publisher, *Electronic Musician*

The advent of the piano helped change the baroque period of Bach to the classical period of Mozart and Beethoven. The rich overtones of the saxophone inspired the non-traditional melodies of jazz. The electric guitar launched rock and roll and made possible the ethereal acid music of Jimi Hendrix. And most recently, the microprocessor-controlled drum machines and samplers initiated rap, hip-hop and techno music.

The current marriage of computers and musical instruments offers the greatest palette of sounds and inspirations that has ever existed. Coupled with the new capabilities this combination offers, such as digital recording, automated notation, and unique orchestrations, we appear to be poised for a new renaissance of music over the next generation.

As people's fascination with this new technology settles down and they learn to control and add more expressiveness to the electronic instruments, maybe more of the internal music that exists within us can be creatively released.

Music and technology will continue in their symbiotic relationship and will remain important to every aspect of humanity.

1

Computers, MIDI and Electronic Music

Making Music With Computers

C ombining computers with music is not a new idea—the earliest experiments date back to the '50s. However, the concept really took off in the early 1980s, when computers became affordable and the MIDI standard for connecting electronic instruments and computers was developed. Shortly thereafter, music software was created, and low-cost personal computers became musical collaborators.

Today, creative companies have produced an enormous variety of software, from music-printing programs to compositional aids to sound editing and organizational tools. Taken as a whole, these programs have made the personal computer an invaluable assistant in any home electronic-music studio. This article provides an overview of the use of computers in the music-making process. With this guide under your belt, the remaining articles in this book will give you the detailed information you'll need to use computers in your own musical endeavors.

BASICS

Before exploring the musical applications of computers, let's cover some basic information. First, there are four types of computers, or "platforms," commonly used by musicians: Apple Macintosh, Atari ST, TT, and Falcon030, Commodore Amiga, and IBM PC and compatibles. Each type of computer comes in several varieties, with different levels of computing power (see "Which Computer for Music?," p. 16).

Connecting a computer to a MIDI system requires a *MIDI interface*. The Atari ST, TT, and Falcon030 include a MIDI interface as standard equipment, but with the other platforms you must buy a separate interface. An interface can take the form of an external box that connects to one of the computer's *serial ports* or a circuit board installed in an expansion slot. Either way, the interface includes one or more MIDI In and Out jacks, which allow MIDI data to be sent back and forth between the computer and connected MIDI devices, such as synthesizers and samplers. (For information on these and other pieces of electronic music-making equipment, see "Unveiling the Mystery" on p. 11.)

Most musical applications for computers involve MIDI in some way, so it would be a good idea to brush up on this subject. (See "What is MIDI?," p. 7.)

BY
SCOTT
WILKINSON

SEQUENCING

One of the most common musical uses for a computer is *sequencing*. This application requires little computing power because the amount of information carried over MIDI lines is relatively low, but it provides a lot of musical options.

By recording the *sequence* of MIDI messages (which result from such performance gestures as playing keys on a keyboard, hitting drum pads, stepping on a sustain pedal, etc.) on different "tracks," a sequencer program simulates a multitrack tape deck within the computer. Put another way, a sequencer lets you record individual musical parts, or "tracks," and combine them to create a complete piece of music.

The MIDI messages which make up these tracks can be edited and manipulated in a wide variety of ways. They also can be sent to MIDI instruments, which respond as if their own keyboards were being played directly. (For more details about the concept and process of sequencing, see "Understanding Sequencing," p. 35.)

Quite a few sequencer programs are available for the four common platforms. Among them are Opcode's *EZ-Vision* and *Vision* and Mark of the Unicorn's *Performer* for the Mac; Steinberg's *Cubase* for the Mac, Atari, and PC-compatibles; Dr. T's *KCS* and *Tiger Cub* for the Atari and Amiga; The Blue Ribbon SoundWorks' *Bars&Pipes Professional* for the Amiga; and Twelve Tone's *Cakewalk* (see **Fig. 1.1**) and Voyetra's *Sequencer Plus* for PC-compatibles.

A variation of sequencing called *algorithmic composition* generates new musical phrases or whole compositions based on parameters you specify. For example, you might play a single phrase into the computer, which then repeats the phrase and alters it in real time as you play something else. Programs that provide these capabilities include Dr. T's *M* for the Mac, Atari, and Amiga; and *Jam Factory* for the Mac.

Another variation is called *automatic accompaniment*. This capability lets you type in the chord changes to any song, and the computer then generates bass, drum, and rhythm parts in a style that you select from a menu. Some programs even include a sequencer that lets you record your own parts along with the accompaniment. Such programs include PG Music's *Band-in-a-Box* for the Mac, Atari, and PC-compatibles; Soundtrek's *The Jammer* for PC-compatibles; and Blue Ribbon's *Super Jam* for the Amiga.

NOTATION

One of the first things most musicians try to do with a computer is transcribe a performance and print music notation. Unfortunately, music notation is very complex, and no program yet exists that can perfectly transcribe what you play. Depending on what you want to do, using notation software can be more frustrating and time-consuming than writing music out by hand. Also, unless you read music, these programs are virtually useless; they don't provide a shortcut for untrained musicians.

But notation programs also can be quite useful. Those of us with illegible hand notation are spared the embarrassment of exposing our written music to other musicians. Also, individual parts can be extracted

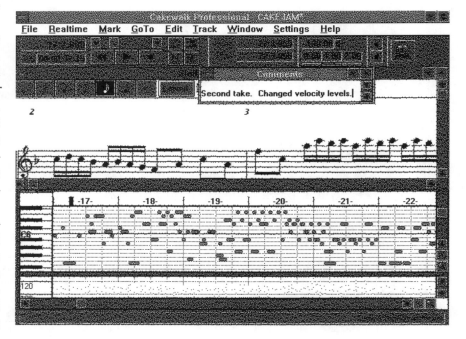

from a score with a minimum of fuss and bother. Notation programs also allow relatively easy transposition, in case your clarinet part must be read by an alto sax player. Word-processing functions such as cut-and-paste and global editing make certain tasks far easier than taking pen or pencil to manuscript paper.

Most notation programs let you enter music in either of two ways: directly, or by importing a sequence file. Direct entry is accomplished using the computer keyboard and/or mouse, or by playing on the MIDI keyboard. Most programs are also able to transcribe sequence files, particularly those in the Standard MIDI File format. (For more about Standard MIDI Files, see p. 55.)

Figure 1.1 Twelve Tone Systems' *Cakewalk for Windows* sequencer for PC-compatibles. The lower portion of the screen is displaying notes in a "piano-roll" format, above which are notes in standard notation.

Fueled by the dreams of musicians everywhere, many companies have developed good notation programs (see **Fig. 1.2**). These include Passport's *Encore* and Coda's *Finale* and *MusicProse* for the Mac and PC-compatibles; Emagic's *Notator* for the Atari; Dr. T's *The Copyist* for Atari, Amiga, and PC-compatibles; and Temporal Acuity Products' *Music Printer Plus* for PC-compatibles. (For more about computer notation, see "Choosing Notation Software" on p. 67 and "Using Notation Software" on p. 75.)

HARD-DISK RECORDING

As personal computers have become more powerful and memory and hard-disk storage less expensive, recording digital audio onto a hard disk has become practical for home studios. (At 10 MB a minute for CD-quality stereo, though, you still need a huge hard disk for any serious work.)

Hard-disk recording systems use an *analog-to-digital converter* (A/D converter) to convert an incoming analog audio signal into digital format. It sends the signal directly to the hard disk, creating a *sound file*. The incoming signal is often already in digital form, when it comes from a DAT or CD player with direct digital outputs. Many systems include digital inputs for this purpose.

Once on disk, the sound file can be edited and manipulated on the screen in ways that would be impossible with analog tape recordings (see **Fig. 1.3**). Digital audio files can be edited using cut-and-paste, transposition, digital signal processing (DSP) such as reverb and EQ, and many other functions. To hear the sound file, the signal is converted back into analog form by a *digital-to-analog converter* (D/A converter or DAC) and played through speakers. The file also may be transferred directly to a DAT without leaving the digital domain.

Many personal computer-based hard-disk recorders are limited to two tracks of playback, due to the speed at which data can be retrieved from a hard disk; there can be no delays while sending digital audio data from the hard disk to the DAC. However, many systems let you assemble multiple tracks of digital audio and select the parts of each track you wish to play at any particular time. You also can mix a sev-

eral tracks down to two within the computer without the sonic degradation that accompanies analog tape mixdowns.

Common hard-disk recording systems include Digidesign's Sound Tools and Pro Tools (a 4- to 16-track system) for the Mac; SunRize Industries' Studio 16 for the Amiga; and Turtle Beach's 56K and Spectral Synthesis' The Digital Studio (4 to 16 tracks) for PC-compatibles. Several companies have combined MIDI sequencing and hard-disk recording into integrated packages. These systems include Opcode's *Studio Vision* and Mark of the Unicorn's *Digital Performer* for the Mac. (For more about hard-disk recording, see p. 87.)

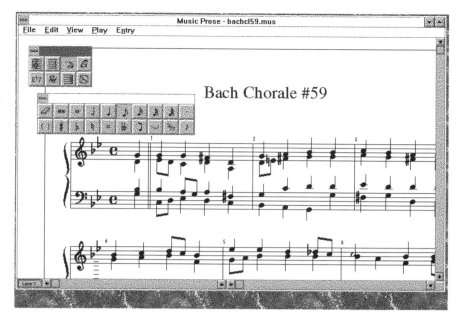

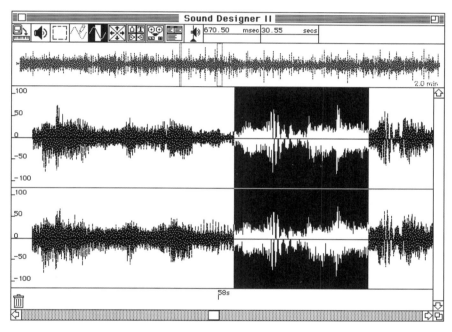

Figure 1.2 (top) Coda's *MusicProse* notation software for PC-compatibles. The symbols in the upper left portion of the screen provide access to common music notation elements.

Figure 1.3 (bottom) Digidesign's Sound Tools hard-disk recording system for the Mac uses the company's *Sound Designer II* software. The inverse-highlighted area is selected for editing.

EDITOR/LIBRARIANS

Most synthesizers have user interfaces that are notoriously difficult to use, due to the button arrangement and small display as well as the complex procedures required to program new sounds. In addition, it can be extremely bothersome to organize bunches of sounds on RAM cards or even floppy disks using the instruments themselves.

Computers offer a superior alternative to programming, storing, and organizing sounds in the form of *editor/librarian* software. These programs display all the instrument's parameters at once on a large screen, in a more or less logical organization. Some parameters such as envelopes are displayed in graphic form, allowing you to use the mouse and drag them into new shapes.

Once a sound has been modified to your liking, it can be stored in a "library" file containing many banks of sounds organized any way you wish. For example, you could store all your bass sounds in one bank and all your brass sounds in another bank. Alternatively, you might want to store all the sounds for one song in a bank.

The parameter values and banks are transferred between the instrument and the computer using MIDI *System Exclusive* messages, which represent the specifics of each individual instrument. This used to mean that you needed a separate editor/librarian program for each instrument in your studio. Such instrument-specific programs include Dr. T's *Caged Artist* series and Sound Quest's *Midi Quest* series for all four platforms, and Turtle Beach's *Oview* series for PC-compatibles, among many others. Most companies now offer *universal editor/librarians* that can be customized to address different instruments within a single program (see **Fig. 1.4**). These include Dr. T's *X-oR* for the PC, ST, and Amiga; Opcode's *Galaxy Plus Editors* for the Mac; and Blue Ribbon's *The PatchMeister* for the Amiga.

Sample editors provide many of the same functions for samplers. These programs fetch samples from the instrument, display the waveforms on the screen, provide editing functions such as looping, trimming, filtering, and envelopes, and return the sample to an instrument. Popular sample editors include Passport's *Alchemy* for the Mac, Steinberg's *Avalon* for the Atari, and Turtle Beach's *SampleVision* for PC-compatibles.

A variation of patch and sample editing is called *software synthesis*. Such programs provide software "modules," such as oscillators, sample players, filters, envelope generators, mixers, and other modifiers, that you assemble and connect on the screen, much like the old modular synthesizers. The resulting "sound" is calculated and stored as a sample, which can be sent to a sampler or played with lower fidelity from the computer's internal speaker. Software synthesis programs include Digidesign's *Turbosynth* for the Mac.

EDUCATION

If you're new to music, you can learn everything from note names and basic rhythm to functional harmony using *computer-aided instruction* (CAI) programs. Ibis Software offers *Take Note, Rhythm Ace*, and several other titles for PC-compatibles; Imaja has *Listen* for the Mac; and Educational Courseware Systems and Temporal Acuity Products have large catalogs of CAI software for various platforms. To learn about MIDI, check out Opcode's *The Book of MIDI*, a HyperCard stack for the Mac.

Despite the headaches computers bring into our lives, they are invaluable tools that help electronic musicians organize their ideas and realize their potential. ♪

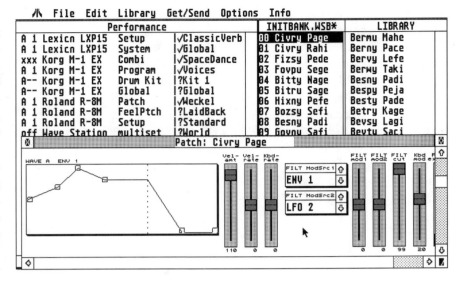

Figure 1.4 Dr. T's *X-oR* universal patch editor/librarian for the Atari ST. In this screen the Performance window displays available devices, while the Voice Edit screen is set up for the Korg Wavestation.

What is MIDI?

M IDI (pronounced midee), the Musical Instrument Digital Interface, can expand your computer's features to rival those of professional recording studios. You can use it to put a veritable orchestra under your fingers by connecting a digital keyboard to your personal computer. With the appropriate music software, you can even do things like print out any notes you play in standard music notation, or teach yourself to play.

Using MIDI need not be difficult, but like music it requires practice and patience to master. This article will describe the basics of MIDI. Don't worry if you don't get everything the first time through. Once you've played with MIDI a bit, parts that seem unclear at first will come into focus. Let's dig in.

THE DEFINITION

MIDI is a standardized protocol that allows computers, electronic keyboards, synthesizers, and other sound-generating modules to communicate and share information. The information they share consists of computer data-like messages that describe various elements of a musical performance: the notes you play, the strength or loudness with which you play them, the particular sound being used, etc. MIDI does not rep-

resent the sound of an instrument; instead, it functions as a common language for sharing the intricacies of performance between various electronic instruments (see sidebar, "What MIDI Isn't"). By itself, MIDI achieves nothing; its sole purpose is to communicate between devices.

MIDI appears as a round, five-pin connector on the backs of products that transmit or receive these messages. There are three types of MIDI connectors or jacks: MIDI In, MIDI Out, and MIDI Thru (see **Fig. 1.5**). MIDI In jacks receive data from other MIDI instruments, MIDI Out jacks transmit data generated by a MIDI instrument, and MIDI Thru jacks retransmit an exact copy of the data that comes into an instrument's MIDI In jack. The MIDI messages are carried by special cables with the five-pin connectors on each end. MIDI messages only travel in one direction, so it's important to make the proper connections. Logically, the order of connection is MIDI Out to MIDI In, or MIDI Thru to MIDI In.

Most instruments and related MIDI accessories are capable of sending and receiving MIDI messages, but they usually perform only one of these functions at a time. Devices which send MIDI data are called "masters" or "controllers," and devices which receive and respond to MIDI messages are "slaves."

BY BOB O'DONNELL

WHY MIDI?

MIDI was developed by professional synthesizer manufacturers as a means for remotely controlling multiple sounds from a single keyboard. By hooking up other keyboards equipped with different sounds, MIDI messages you generate by playing the master keyboard can "play" the connected instruments at the same time. To offer more sonic variety to musicians at a reasonable cost, instrument manufacturers also created keyboardless sound modules, whose sole purpose is to respond to MIDI messages they receive from MIDI keyboards or computers and generate sounds. These devices contain the sound-generating circuitry of a keyboard in a more compact, generally less-expensive package.

MIDI messages also can be recorded into a type of computer program known as a *sequencer*, where they can be altered, added to, or subtracted from, and played back at a later time (see "Understanding Sequencing," p. 35). Most sequencers offer numerous simultaneous "tracks," or places to record MIDI messages. By combining these tracks with the ability to play back previously recorded material, you can create complete compositions with piano, bass, drums, strings, brass, and more, one part at a time. In other words, you could record a piano part on one track, and then (while listening to that part) add a bass line onto another track, then add strings, etc. MIDI offers this capability by spreading its messages across 16 MIDI channels (numbered 1-16). Messages for each instrument need to be on their own channel (otherwise you'll hear multiple instruments playing the same part), but all sixteen channels are carried over a single MIDI cable. In this example, the piano could be sent on channel one, bass on channel two, strings on channel five, etc.

If your keyboard is multitimbral, meaning it's capable of responding to multiple MIDI channels and playing multiple sounds at once, you can have many or all of the parts played on the keyboard. If it's not, you can connect a multitimbral MIDI sound module to the keyboard with MIDI cables and use the sound module to play the other instrument sounds. If you're using a computer that's running a sequencing program, you would connect the sound module directly to the computer or to the keyboard's

MIDI Thru jack. By using the MIDI Thru, the sound module will receive an exact duplicate of the messages the keyboard receives from the computer. In either case, you will not hear any sound from the sound module unless you also connect its audio outputs to the keyboard's auxiliary inputs or to a small sound system. MIDI cables do not carry audio, only MIDI messages.

Building up numerous musical parts with a sequencer is great fun, but eventually you may run out of voices. For example, unlike a real piano, most MIDI instruments can play only 8, 16 or 32 notes at once. If you're asking them to play all the parts in a song, those notes can get used up quickly. If you do run out, you'll need to simplify your music or get an external sound module, which generally offers sixteen or more of its own voices along with the keyboard's voices.

HOW DOES IT WORK?

MIDI works like an elaborate remote-control system. If you play a note on a MIDI keyboard, for example, it generates a message that is sent to the MIDI Out connector. That message then travels down a MIDI cable to any other connected piece of MIDI equipment. Upon receiving the message, the connected device identifies the message and responds accordingly. If the receiving device is another synthesizer, for example, it will play the same note— but not necessarily the same sound—as the one played on the transmitting keyboard. If a piece of equipment is not designed to handle a particular type of MIDI message (or is set to receive on a different MIDI channel), it ignores the message and

Figure 1.5 The three types of MIDI jacks: In, Out, and Thru.

does nothing. MIDI does not add new capabilities to equipment; it simply provides a way to take advantage of the features already included.

MESSAGES

To understand MIDI messages, it helps to think of MIDI as a means of translating musical performance into a digital form. Again, MIDI does not contain nor have anything to do with audio signals; rather, it consists of performance gestures (such as playing a particular note, selecting a particular sound, moving a pitch bend wheel, etc.).

Most messages in the MIDI protocol describe specific performance-oriented actions, though they need not be "performed" or even generated by a human player. With a *sequencer*, for example, you can enter one MIDI message at a time and then have the computer play it back. Among MIDI's messages are *Note On*, which tells a connected instrument to play a certain note at a certain "velocity," or loudness level; *Program Change*, which tells a connected device to switch to a different sound or patch; and *MIDI continuous controllers*, such as *Pitch Bend* and *MIDI Volume*, which describe continuous changes in the pitch and level of individual sounds.

Every performance message is assigned to one of MIDI's sixteen channels. For a piece of equipment to respond to a message from another MIDI device, the two must be set to receive and send on the same MIDI channel. This is an important but often overlooked point, so save yourself some trouble by remembering it: Merely connecting two MIDI devices properly *does not* guarantee communication between the two. You need to make sure that the devices are using the same MIDI channel, or channels in the case of a *multitimbral* instrument.

MIDI MORE

Though it is primarily used by, and was created for, keyboards, MIDI also works with numerous other instrument controllers. Today, you can find MIDI guitars, MIDI drum pads, MIDI saxophones, MIDI violins, and more. These vary in the way they are played, but they share the ability to generate MIDI messages (just like those from a keyboard) that can control other MIDI instruments. If you want to play

drums from a guitar, or piano from electronic drum pads, you just connect the MIDI output of the desired controller to the desired receiver's input and jam to your heart's content.

MIDI messages also can be used to control devices that are not musical instruments, including stage lighting systems and even tape recorders. Because MIDI is simply a command language used to send messages to receiving devices—which can then respond in any number of ways—the possibilities are practically limitless.

THE COMPUTER CONNECTION

MIDI speaks a digital language similar to the one used by computers, so the combination of MIDI instruments and computers was obvious. You don't *need* a computer to take advantage of MIDI, but using one in conjunction with MIDI offers many powerful options. To use a computer with MIDI equipment, you need a MIDI interface for your type of computer (unless you own an Atari ST, TT or Falcon030, which

WHAT MIDI ISN'T

As important as it may be to understand what MIDI is it's even more important that you understand what MIDI is not: MIDI is not audio. No matter how many MIDI cables you have hooked up, you won't get any sound unless an audio output is connected to an amplifier and speaker.

It's also important to realize that you can't listen to MIDI directly. You might as well try to listen to a piano roll without a player piano. There always must be some kind of sound-generating device to respond to the messages in the MIDI "score." MIDI messages will tell a slaved instrument to play at the appropriate time, but they have no way of knowing if the slave instrument has been connected.

Another common point of confusion involves *Program Change*, a type of MIDI message. People sometimes get the idea that selecting a certain type of sound on the master keyboard will cause any slaved instruments to switch to the same kind of sound, but this is not necessarily true. A Program Change message—generated when you select a new sound—merely tells receiving devices to select the appropriately numbered program. If you select program 23 on the master controller, the receiving device will call up its own patch number 23, without regard for the nature of that sound.

A new addition to the MIDI specification that standardizes patch-to-instrument assignments, called General MIDI, was recently adopted, but most current digital keyboards don't adhere to it. With two General MIDI-compliant instruments, patch number 1 always calls up Acoustic Piano, 47 always calls up strings, etc. Look for this to become a standard feature of MIDI keyboards and sound modules in the near future. (For more on General MIDI, see p. 49.)

have them built in) to translate MIDI messages into a form that computers understand directly. Numerous manufacturers offer MIDI interfaces for the PC, Mac, Amiga, and other computers.

A computer and the appropriate MIDI software (not all music software requires or even supports MIDI, by the way) allow you to do many things with the MIDI data your keyboard generates. In addition to sequencing programs, there are music notation packages that can transcribe what you play into standard music notation and then print it out. Other programs allow you to edit existing sounds or create new ones for certain keyboards and sound modules, teach you how to play, provide sophisticated auto-accompaniment, teach basic principles of ear training and music theory, and more.

CONCLUSION

In its few years of existence, MIDI has greatly contributed to the growth and expanded capabilities of electronic musical instruments. Musicians around the world, working in living rooms, bedrooms, and professional recording studios of all shapes and sizes, now use MIDI to help bring their musical ideas to life. In the truest sense, it has brought about a revolution. Use it to create your own. ♪

Unveiling the Mystery: The Basics of Electronic Music

BY DAN PHILLIPS

If you're just getting started in electronic music, you may find yourself wading through a morass of buzzwords—multitimbral, polyphony, looping, quantization, graphic editing, etc.—that seem to have little or no connection to music-making. Too often, articles and manufacturers' brochures assume you already understand terms and ideas that aren't self-explanatory. Don't be intimidated; most of the fundamental ideas aren't as difficult as they appear at first. With a little effort and a solid dose of patience, you can learn the basics, start selecting your gear, and get on with making music.

The electronic music-making process can be explained in terms of two broad categories: the equipment used to create and play sounds and the tools used to organize the sounds into complete musical compositions. Electronic music systems of today most often include elements of both.

Electric and amplified acoustic instruments generate sound acoustically, using strings, reeds, and other devices that directly cause wave vibrations in the air. There are several ways—magnetic pickups and microphones are two common examples—to convert the sonic waves into an analogous electrical signal whose waveform is a copy of the sound wave. Electronic (as distinguished from "electric") musical instruments don't create sound *per se*; they use a circuit to generate the electrical signals directly. A sound is only created when a speaker transforms the electrical signal into sound waves.

The archetypal electronic musical instrument is the synthesizer. Synthesis is a broad term that refers to the creation of sound by any electronic technique. Because their sound is generated "synthetically," rather than "naturally," electronic instruments were dubbed "synthesizers." The structure and sounds of synthesizers vary widely. Some have their own keyboards, some don't.

Synthesizers are characterized by malleability: Because the sound is created from scratch, it can be modified (modulated) drastically, even as the instrument is being played. The strength of synthesis is that wild, dramatic, and often otherworldly sounds can be created easily, and a variety of techniques can be used to bring a sense of dynamics and "animation" to sounds. A weakness (if it can be considered that) is that the sounds are often manifestly electronic, and it can be difficult to realistically simulate the sounds of familiar instruments.

SAMPLING AND SAMPLE PLAYBACK

If you wish to use the sounds of acoustic instruments such as piano, guitar, brass, or orchestral strings, sampling technology is

11

the way to go. Instruments with sampling capabilities can faithfully recreate complex timbres that are difficult or impossible to achieve with current synthesis methods.

A sample is a short recording of sound, just like the recordings on CDs or cassettes. It may be the sound of a single flute playing a quiet B-flat, or the sound of thunder in a downpour. Today's sampler is a microprocessor-based device that records sounds either with a microphone or directly from a line-level sound source (such as a CD player or tape deck), stores them as digital (computer) data, and plays them back each time a controller is triggered. The sample is played back at different rates to transpose the original recording to the desired pitch (just like changing the speed of a record player), so that a single sample can be played across a musical keyboard.

This method works well, but transposing an instrument by too large an interval can seriously distort the nature of the sound. To prevent this effect, several recordings of different pitches are used to cover the full range of the instrument. Most sample-based instruments use this technique, which is known as multisampling.

Samplers (see **Fig. 1.6**) allow you to record sounds of your own as well. This gives you extra flexibility, but sampling is a difficult and time-consuming art, and you should make sure you have a real need for this capability. Samplers often are considerably more expensive than instruments that merely play back pre-recorded sample libraries, and there are excellent (and extensive) libraries available. The payoff, of course, is that you won't be limited to pre-recorded sounds. If you want to fold, spindle, and mutilate recorded sound (after the manner of rap and musique concréte), samplers are the way to go. In any case, you should be prepared to spend a lot more time organizing and tweaking your sound materials if you use a "real" sampler.

A popular type of instrument today is the so-called "sample-playback synth," which plays back pre-recorded (sampled) sounds and usually includes many of the sound-processing capabilities of synthesis (see **Fig. 1.7**). On some older instruments (such as the Mellotron, made famous by

the Beatles), the sound actually was recorded on a piece of tape that was played each time a particular key was hit. Modern machines generally contain a sizable library of sampled sounds in permanent computer memory so you can start playing music immediately at power-up. Some sample-playback machines let you add more sounds from a computer, or with memory cards or chips, but they can't record audio. Because sample-playback instruments combine many of the strengths of sampling (real sounds) with those of synthesis (malleability), these instruments often prove to be the best of both worlds and are an excellent choice for the first-time buyer.

Many drum machines and piano modules also use sample-playback technology (although some use synthesized sounds). Drum machines usually include their own sequencers (discussed later), which allow them to produce not just sounds, but complete rhythmic grooves. Although general-purpose sample-playback devices usually include drums and piano sounds, you may get higher quality with an instrument dedicated to a specific purpose, and many of these are attractively priced. If you intend to use piano or drums extensively, it may be worth your while to investigate these dedicated modules.

Figure 1.6 The Akai S950 is a sampler capable of recording, editing and playing back sounds.

Figure 1.7 The E-mu Proteus is a sample playback synth whose built-in sampled sounds cannot be changed by the user, although they can be manipulated in many ways. Both are designed to be played via MIDI.

CONTROLLERS

One critical concept in electronic music is that the device that makes a sound is separate from the device the performer uses to play the sound. The most common "controller" today is the piano-style keyboard. Many synths and samplers include their own keyboards, but a keyboard is a triggering mechanism, not the part that makes actual sounds. In other words, a keyboard synthesizer consists of two components combined into one: a keyboard controller and a sound source. Many instruments omit the keyboard entirely and are designed to be played from external controllers (keyboard or otherwise). These "sound modules" often come in the form of rackmount boxes. The combination of a controller and sound module is functionally equivalent to a keyboard with built-in sounds.

When a key is pressed on a modern keyboard controller, a MIDI message is sent to the sound source (whether synth or sampler) that tells the source to play the appropriate note. When the key is lifted, another MIDI message is sent that tells the sound source to stop playing.

Keyboards are by no means the only kind of controller (although they are certainly the most common). Electronic instruments can be played using guitar controllers; wind controllers that resemble saxophones, recorders, or clarinets; percussion controllers (see **Fig. 1.8**); computer controllers (joystick, keyboard, mouse, etc.); and a variety of unconventional instruments. These devices produce no sound of their own, but generate messages that are used to "play" remote sound modules and control an ever-increasing selection of other devices, including mixers and effects processors.

You can remote-control a fair-sized studio from a keyboard, computer, or other controller by connecting the controller to the sound modules and other gear with MIDI. In brief, MIDI is a way for electronic musical equipment of many types (including personal computers) to exchange messages over standardized cables. MIDI can do far more than just trigger sound modules; as you'll see, it's the source of an enormous amount of musical power.

Non-keyboard ("alternative") controllers often allow the performer a good deal of

real-time ("live") control over timbre, rivaling the expressive control of conventional acoustic instruments. This control has a huge impact on the character of the sound. I once heard a friend play a MIDI wind controller solo that I would have sworn was played with a real saxophone (see **Fig. 1.9**). When I asked him what sampler he used to create such a realistic effect, I found that he used a very inexpensive synthesizer. His playing, especially his skilled use of the instrument's pitch bend and breath control, made the difference between a cheap imitation and compelling, expressive realism.

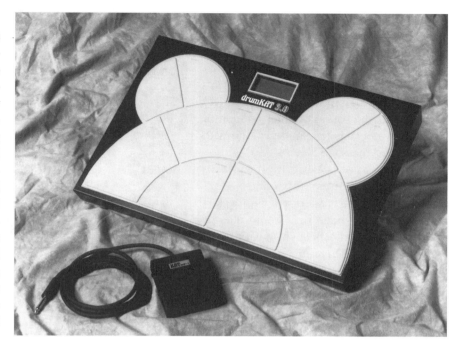

Figure 1.8 When struck with drumsticks, the DrumKat generates MIDI messages that can be used to trigger drum and percussion sounds.

Figure 1.9 The Yamaha WX-11 MIDI wind controller with the WT-11, a synthesizer designed to complement the WX-11.

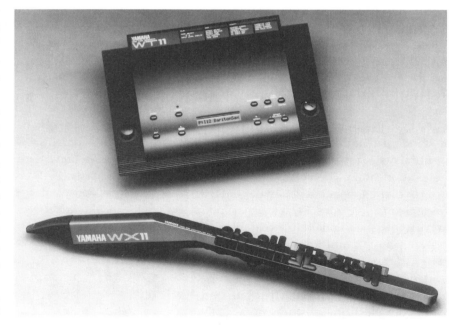

MIDI keyboards are not without their own expressive capabilities, however. Many instruments feature velocity sensitivity: The faster a key is pressed down, the greater that note's velocity. Typically, the synth or sampler sound is programmed so that higher velocities make the sound brighter, louder, or both. The velocity is transmitted along with the "note-on" message.

In addition to velocity, many instruments offer aftertouch ("pressure") control. This triggers when you press down on the key after the note has been struck, and often is used for adding effects such as vibrato or orchestral swells. There are two variations: When you trigger channel aftertouch, pressing one key affects all keys; polyphonic aftertouch affects only the key(s) triggered.

Wheels (see **Fig. 1.10**) or joysticks can be used to bend a pitch up or down, or perform other modifications of the sound (depending on how you program the controller and the synth or sampler). They're often used to introduce vibrato, the effect a violinist obtains by wiggling his/her finger on a string. Breath controllers (small, whistle-like devices that the player blows into) are less common but very effective, especially for emulations of wind and brass instruments.

Pitch Bend, Modulation, and Breath Control are standardized messages that can be transmitted over MIDI and are recognized by most sound-producing modules. A number of other controllers, including pedals, sliders, and switches, are supported by various instruments. Since these controls can be changed after a note has been struck, they enable the musician to shape the timbre of a note or phrase in ways not possible with acoustic keyboard instruments.

POLYPHONIC VERSUS MULTITIMBRAL

A standard feature of modern electronic instruments is the ability to play multiple notes at one time. This seems obvious, but not so long ago synthesizers were limited to single melodic lines. Even today, synths and samplers are limited in the number of polyphonic (simultaneous) notes, or "voices," they can produce. This is an important factor to consider when selecting an instrument for your particular purpose.

Current electronic instruments usually have somewhere between sixteen- and 32-voice polyphony. This may seem to be a

lot, but multiple voices often are combined to produce thicker, richer, and more interesting sounds, greatly reducing the number of notes available.

Most instruments today also provide the ability to produce different sounds (timbres) at the same time. In essence, they work as several independent instruments in one. This "multitimbral" capability is especially important when using sequencing (discussed later) to compose music with multiple instrumental parts. Multitimbral use puts much greater demands on the polyphonic capacity of an instrument. Because these separate sounds are produced by a single device, they are known as "virtual instruments," existing in function but not in physical space.

Multitimbral sound generators allow independent control of each of these virtual instruments as if each one had its own keyboard. MIDI provides this ability by addressing each virtual instrument on any of sixteen separate MIDI "channels." Every MIDI message sent by a controller contains an "address" that defines the MIDI channel. Notes received are

Figure 1.10 Pitch bend and modulation wheels can add expression to MIDI keyboard controller performance.

Figure 1.11 The Alesis Quadraverb GT combines several effects for guitarists in a single, programmable rack unit.

only played by an instrument that has been assigned to that channel. Multitimbral sound modules are able to receive on multiple MIDI channels, allowing each virtual instrument to play separately. If you are interested in using a sequencer to create a "band at your fingertips" (see below), multitimbral instruments can be extremely valuable.

Even in "live" performance, many instruments allow you to *layer* and *split* different sounds. In layering, two different, complementary sounds are played together whenever a key is depressed. This is useful for creating rich, complex sounds. You might, for instance, layer a bell sound with strings for a ballad, combine strings with brass for an orchestral effect, or blend nameless synth sounds to get a huge new timbre.

Splitting a keyboard means that, instead of playing all of the sounds on each key, the keyboard is divided into ranges, each of which plays a different sound. The range from the lowest C to B below middle C, for instance, might be assigned to play a bass sound, while middle C to the top of the keyboard might trigger an electric piano.

SIGNAL PROCESSING

Effects and other types of signal processing are an integral part of electronic music production (see **Fig. 1.11**). Most people have found that judicious use of processing greatly enhances the effect that electronic sounds have on the listener. Think of such processing as the icing on the cake, the finishing touch that brings extra life to a sound.

Reverberation is the most commonly used form of processing. It is frequently used to add realism and a sense of space to electronic sound. Used in large amounts, the effect is the kind of washy decay that you hear after clapping your hands in a large room or singing in a stairwell. Used more subtly, reverberation simply gives the impression that a sound has been performed in real space.

Delay is sometimes confused with reverb and consists of one or more discrete repetitions of the original sound. At longer delay times (a half-second or more), the effect is like hearing echoes across a canyon. At shorter times, delay can enhance the rhythmic qualities of a sound, while still shorter times can be used to "thicken" the sound or increase the listener's sense of space in a stereo listening situation.

Chorusing introduces slight amounts of detuning into a sound, making it thicker and warmer. String sections and choirs, which feature a number (a chorus) of sound sources that are slightly out of tune, were the inspiration for this effect.

Distortion, so often coupled with guitars, is an example of signal processing that takes the original sound in a completely new direction. Used judiciously, distortion effects can add an organic sense to synthesized textures. By introducing small amounts of chaos into sound, it can be made to seem more dynamic, full of motion.

There are many excellent and affordable effects modules on the market. Some of these stand-alone devices provide only one type of signal processing, while others can produce any of a number of different effects, from reverb to distortion—or even several different effects at once. Today, many instruments include built-in effects as part of the sound-producing process.

SOUND SYSTEMS

Finally, your electronic-music setup will need some sort of sound system to make the results of your hard work audible. If you're only using a single MIDI instrument, this can be as simple as a pair of headphones, a home stereo, or a pair of computer or instrument speakers with a built-in amplifier. For MIDI setups with more than one instrument, you should plan on adding a mixer, which will allow you to combine and balance the sounds of several individual instruments. A basic mixer is fine for simple systems, but a more sophisticated unit will let you work with many individual instruments and effects units.

IN CONCLUSION...

These days, a personal computer forms the center of many electronic music systems. Computers can control as much of the production process—creating and triggering sounds, signal processing, mixing, and recording—as your knowledge and budget permit.

Although the concepts of modern electronic music are not exceptionally difficult, the many terms used to describe them are often a source of confusion. I hope I've clarified a few of the more important pieces of jargon so that you're able to get more out of your purchasing dollar and more into your music. ♪

Which Computer for Music?

BY
BOB
O'DONNELL

*O*nce a luxury, now a necessity." As it does for many aspects of modern life, this phrase captures the relationship between computers and electronic music quite well. Whether your interests lie in composing, recording, or performing at the amateur or professional level, a computer has become an indispensable part of the music-making process. Over the last few years, computers have taken on the roles of recorder, editor, librarian, compositional assistant, arranger, and copyist, and the job list keeps growing.

But while the computer's stature and functions are clear, it's not as obvious which type is best suited for these musical roles. Of the many choices, how do you determine which platform has the best built-in audio capabilities, the best hardware options, and most importantly, the best music- and audio-related software?

There is no simple answer. IBM PCs and compatibles, Apple Macintoshes, Atari STs, TTs, and the Falcon030, Commodore Amigas, and UNIX-based personal workstations such as the NeXT computer and Silicon Graphics' IRIS Indigo offer different benefits and suffer from different shortcomings. And after you decide on a computer type, you still must answer the (often more difficult) question of which model.

Even if you already own a computer, you're not saved from considering whether it's *enough* computer. New, powerful applications often devour memory and processing power, and keeping pace with your increasing desires may require trading up to a beefier machine.

Unfortunately, new computer hardware isn't cheap, and buying a computer for music isn't like purchasing one to do a little word-processing. The questions are much more complex.

Of course, the most important consideration when purchasing a computer, or any gear, is determining what you plan to do with it. If your interest is in hard-disk recording, you'll need more power than someone who wants to do some basic sequencing. A computer is an investment (albeit a rapidly depreciating one), so think about the long term. Sequencing and notation may be fine for now, but a computer-based hard-disk recording system may not be far off.

Considering future needs requires addressing other tough questions: Can the computer support the I/O throughput necessary for hard-disk recording? Are multi-port MIDI interfaces available for it? (See "Multi-port MIDI Interfaces," p. 30.) Can it produce PostScript printed output? (See "Choosing a Printer for Music Notation," p. 72.) Does the system software support multitasking? Find the answers to these and other relevant concerns, peek into your bank account, and you'll be well on your way to figuring out which computer is best for your music-making efforts.

SOFTWARE, SOFTWARE, SOFTWARE

Common wisdom dictates that software should determine your choice of computer. In other words, select the software you want to use and then buy the computer on which it runs. For example, if you want to use *Performer*, you need a Mac, for *Bars&Pipes* an Amiga, for *Notator* an ST, and for *Cakewalk* a PC. However, while still basically valid, this advice is no longer sacrosanct, as several major music applications such as *Finale, MasterTracks Pro, Cubase, MIDI Quest, Band-In-A-Box* and *KCS* run on multiple platforms. (Note that programs running on multiple platforms are not always identical. For example, system-level idiosyncrasies often prompt slight variations in Mac and PC versions of the same program.)

If you have a broad range of musical interests, it's important to know the total number of music applications available per platform. In the U.S., the most programs are available for PCs and compatibles, with the Mac second, the Atari ST a close third, and the Amiga languishing behind. Both the NeXT and Silicon Graphics machines currently have minimal commercial music software, but that situation should change gradually.

More importantly, you'll want to consider several specific software applications when choosing a computer.

• **Sequencing** For most electronic musicians, the most important application is sequencing. (See "Understanding Sequencing," p. 35.) Sequencers function as excellent composing and arranging tools, and consequently play a very important role in most systems. If you're going to base your decision on any one piece of software, make it your sequencer.

In general, the most sophisticated sequencers are available on the Mac and ST, but there are many excellent choices for the PC as well. PC users should pay particular attention to the growing legion of *Windows* sequencers.

• **Notation** If you want to print out your music or compose it with a comput-

Commodore Amiga 3000

erized version of a traditional score, you'll want to investigate notation software (which some classically trained musicians use as their primary tool). The most sophisticated programs are available for the Mac and PC, but there are PostScript-capable programs on the ST and Amiga as well. The PC has the widest range of programs, offering several inexpensive options and a few expensive, complicated systems, but the Mac's consistent graphical interface really helps when working with music notation. (See "Choosing Notation Software," p. 67.)

• **Editor/Librarian** To store and edit all the patches in your synthesizers, you'll want an editor/librarian program (or just a librarian if you're not interested in programming). Several companies market programs for individual instruments or processors. However, financially you're much better off going with a universal program that works with many instruments—as long as the products you own are supported, of course. Universal programs are available on all four main platforms, but the Mac, ST, and Amiga are your best choices if you desire graphic editing of synth parameters.

If you own a sampler or one of the newer synths that supports user samples and the MIDI Sample Dump Standard, a sample-editing program is extremely handy. These offer graphic depictions of sampled waveforms and allow you to manipulate them to your heart's content. Software of this type originated on the Mac, but sophisticated options are available on the PC, ST, and Amiga. Along similar lines, programs for creating and synthesizing waveforms for downloading into samplers are available on the Mac and PC, but the ST boasts the most sophisticated package.

• **Other Music Software** Other types of music applications include educational software, algorithmic-composition software, and performance-oriented software. Educational programs range from music theory to piano lessons to ear training. The PC and the venerable Apple II series are well-supported here, with the Mac and ST also offering decent sets of choices. In the realm of algorithmic composition, where the computer acts as a co-composer, all four major platforms have different but equally strong options available. Finally, live performance-oriented software, in which the computer acts as a "co-performer" or a performance enhancer, is best supported on the Mac, though the PC and ST have several strong applications.

GENERAL SOFTWARE ENVIRONMENT

Of course, there's more to life than music software. When working with a computer, you'll first encounter its operating system. This is software that tells the computer how to function. A few years ago, this didn't have much relevance for music software, because most operating systems didn't know or care much about music and audio. Microsoft's *MultiMedia Extensions (MME)* to *Windows* (see p. 113), incorporated into *Windows* 3.1, and Apple's *MIDI Manager* (see p. 25) and *QuickTime* (see p. 115) have changed that by bringing operating system-level support for MIDI and synchronized audio onto the PC and Macintosh platforms.

What this means is that music applications can be written more easily and more effectively for these two platforms. In the long run, this benefits users. In addition, these extensions permit more sophisticated interaction between multiple programs and hardware peripherals, such as controlling internal synthesizer cards from a sequencing program and/or notation program.

To run multiple programs concurrently, an operating system also must be capable of multitasking. The Atari ST's TOS operating system does not support multitasking,

Atari STacy laptop

but the Falcon030 and all the other platforms do. The Macintosh, through *MIDI Manager*, currently is the only platform that allows sophisticated data-sharing, or inter-application communication, between music programs on the system level. Multiple music programs can run simultaneously on the ST and Amiga, but only through proprietary software links.

BUT WHAT ABOUT HARDWARE?

As important a role as software may play in your choice of computer, the hardware cannot be ignored. In fact, as more programs start to cross platforms, the operating system and hardware will become primary influences on the decision to buy one computer over another.

Hardware differences also may determine the specific model you want, once you've settled on a computer type. For example, if you pick the PC, you can select a '286-, '386SX-, '386DX-, '486SX-, or '486DX-based machine with ISA (Industry Standard Architecture), EISA (Extended Industry Standard Architecture), or MicroChannel slots and VGA, Super VGA, or XGA graphics.

• **Physical Design** The first question you need to answer is: portable or stationary? If you're attracted by the sexy new notebook computers, you can choose from PCs, Macs, or the STBook. In the case of PC notebooks, you'll have to work with serial port-based MIDI interfaces such as the one from Key Electronics, because notebooks don't have room for plug-in boards. Mac MIDI interfaces all use the serial port, although the PowerBooks have some compatibility problems with MIDI. The STBook has MIDI In and Out jacks; however, its small size forced Atari to use non-standard mini-sized jacks that require adaptor cables.

If you don't plan on going mobile, choose a desktop or tower model with as many slots as you can. If you buy a PC, you're better off getting 16-bit ISA or 32-bit EISA slots instead of MicroChannel, because almost all MIDI, synthesis, and digital-audio boards are designed to work with the ISA/EISA formats.

Don't overlook display options, either. You'll be staring at your monitor a lot, so it's worth spending more money to find something you really like. Most music applications don't require color, but large screens can be very helpful.

• **Computing Power** The specification most frequently used to rate computers is their microprocessor or CPU (central processing unit). All PCs and compatibles use Intel microprocessors, which are numbered 80x86. Macs, STs, and Amigas all use Motorola-manufactured CPUs, numbered 680x0. In both cases, the higher the number, the faster and more complex the processor. Comparisons across the two lines are more difficult to make, but equal-numbered variables offer approximately equal power (i.e., a PC's 80486 processor is in the same league as a Mac's 68040). One important difference in the Intel line is that SX versions of chips are less powerful than DX versions (Intel/Motorola comparisons are more accurate for DX chips).

The other important specification is processor speed, which is expressed in megahertz (MHz). Early machines ran at 8 and 12 MHz, while newer machines run at 25 and 33 MHz or beyond. Again, the higher the speed, the faster the computer.

Another element that affects computer speed is the presence or absence of a math co-processor (numbered 80x87 for Intel and 68881 or 68882 for Motorola). This chip speeds up complex mathematical operations, such as spreadsheets and digital audio editing. Most high-powered Macs and Amigas and the Atari TT offer this as a standard feature, while it's optional on most PCs.

I'd highly recommend at least a 68030- or 80386-based machine, even if you only plan on doing sequencing. In addition to more processing power for music, these systems support faster graphic redraws and other niceties that make your general computing experience much more pleasant. (They also represent a better investment for the future.) If you plan on doing any hard-disk recording, these models represent the minimum processing power you'll need to make most systems work.

To fulfill these requirements on a Motorola machine, you'll want a Mac Classic II, LCII, IIsi, IIci, IIvx, IIfx, or Quadra; an Amiga 2500, 3000, 3000T, or 4000, or an Atari TT.

Another processor that's becoming increasingly important for sophisticated music and audio applications is a DSP chip, or digital signal processor (such as Motorola's 56001). The NeXT, Silicon Graphics IRIS Indigo, Atari's Falcon 030 and IBM's Ultimedia PS/2 M57 SLC come standard with a DSP chip. However, all plug-in hard-disk recording boards require some type of DSP to perform the demanding processing that recording, editing, and playing back digital audio requires. Look for more mainstream computers to offer DSP as standard, particularly as digital video and multimedia become more prominent.

One commonly overlooked area when choosing a computer is media support: What type of recordable or readable storage media are available for use? If you plan on doing any hard-disk recording, you'll need to be able to work with several-hundred-megabyte hard disks, tape backups, and other removable media. The best and largest storage options are available for the Mac and PC. Also, the Mac, PC, and Amiga are the only mainstream computers that directly support CD-ROM.

• **Expandability** You'll undoubtedly want to expand your computer's capabilities at some point, and the likely first candidate for an upgrade is memory. Four megabytes may seem extravagant at first, but after a while even eight may not be enough. To make upgrading easier and less expensive, you should look for a computer that uses standard SIMMs (Single In-line Memory Modules). All Macs (except the PowerBooks), most PCs, and all STs offer SIMM slots. (TTs require proprietary memory modules.)

The second most likely upgrade is to a bigger hard disk. Make sure you can upgrade an existing internal drive and/or connect another drive.

Finally, find out how the display can be upgraded. After checking out photo-realistic 24-bit color, you may find that 4-bit standard VGA just doesn't cut it. If so, find out whether you need to buy a display adapter board, or if you can simply upgrade the existing hardware.

• **Internal Sound-Generating Capability** When first introduced, the Amiga's 4-channel sound chip was considered quite good, but a few CD-influenced years later it and similar 8-bit sound generators found in the Mac, ST, and MPC-capable PCs just don't stand up. Yes, you can use them for games, voice applications, and perhaps some multimedia presentations, but they won't work for serious music. Also, the 8-bit A/D converters found on the NeXT and Macs, while a good start, don't meet the audio standards our ears have come to expect. Thankfully, things are improving. Atari's Falcon030, Silicon Graphics' Indigo, and many PC sound cards support 16-bit stereo input and output.

• **Hardware Cards** Of course, what isn't standard often can be added via a plug-in card, and there are several available with direct relevance to music and audio. If you select a PC, the most important card you'll need is a MIDI interface. Until recently, PCs were limited to 32 independent MIDI channels (two sets of 16 each), but several manufacturers have introduced or are working on multi-port MIDI interfaces with up to eight independent ports for 128 MIDI channels. Multi-port interfaces also are available for the Mac, ST, and Amiga. (See "Multi-port MIDI Interfaces," p. 30.)

A number of plug-in synthesizer cards, which permit integration of high-quality sound generation into the computer, also have begun to appear. These devices essentially consist of the sound-generating circuitry of a synthesizer or sample-playback device stuffed onto a circuit board. At the moment, boards of this type are available only for the Mac and the PC, partially because they require system-level software support to be seamlessly integrated.

• **Hard-disk Recording** Along similar lines are boards (and accompanying software) that allow recording to hard disk. This is currently the hottest development in electronic music. Early systems allowed you to record two tracks to disk, but newer systems permit up to sixteen channels of hard disk recording on a single computer with multiple large hard drives. The flexibility offered by these types of digital audio editing systems, particularly when combined with MIDI sequencing, allows unprecedented control over every aspect of a musical per-

Macintosh Quadra

formance (see "An Introduction to Hard Disk Recording," p. 87). You will pay for that power, however, in terms of the boards, software, computer, and hard disks required to run these programs.

As mentioned before, these systems typically require a very fast computer, but a few companies have products for the Mac and ST that take a different approach. Instead of using plug-in boards, these systems connect to the computer via hard-disk ports and offload all processing to an external box. This allows digital-audio programs to run on less powerful computers, because the computer only has to worry about sending and receiving messages and updating the screen. If you're locked into less powerful hardware, but you're still interested in hard-disk recording, these systems are an option (though you may want to invest the money in a more powerful computer).

• **Multimedia** If you're interested in producing or viewing multimedia on your computer, you need to consider a new set of criteria. Most importantly, you'll want to investigate hardware and software for viewing, storing, and manipulating video. In the hardware category, several types of video boards are available: those that simply display an analog video signal on a screen, those that digitize and manipulate video in real time (and show it on the computer screen), those that output computer graphics onto videotape, and those that can compress and store video on hard disk. Some boards combine the functionality of several types in one package.

Video software consists of programs that can create video titles to overlay incoming video, process real-time video (in conjunction with a hardware board), and edit digitized video. General graphics programs also can be used to create graphics that can be output to videotape. The major players here are the Amiga, Mac, and PC, though the Silicon Graphics IRIS Indigo promises to make a strong showing.

The final consideration for multimedia producers is authoring software, which allows you to organize and construct a multimedia presentation (see "Making Multimedia," p. 101). Amigas and Macs are the primary forces here, especially with Commodore bundling their *AmigaVision*, but several new entries for *Windows*-equipped MPCs are making inroads as well.

FUTURE GROWTH

Despite all your research, the sad fact is that any computer you currently own or decide to buy will be somewhat, if not completely, outdated within a year. Even if you've got the latest 80486DX- or 68040-based machine, twelve months from now you'll feel a slight twinge of longing for this year's models. Consequently, the final point you should consider when buying or upgrading a computer is an upgrade path. Some manufacturers, such as Atari and many PC clone makers, offer no upgrade path, while others such as Compaq and Dell let you individually upgrade several different components (including the microprocessor). Commodore, Apple, and NeXT lie somewhere in the middle, offering plug-in accelerators or board swaps for similar-sized computers. These upgrades can be rather expensive, but they're definitely less costly than buying a new machine.

CONCLUSION

So which computer is the best for music? Well, it depends on your needs. If you want a good general-purpose machine for sequencing and notation, with a large selection of software, go with the PC. If you'll be working primarily with music software and aren't as concerned about expandability, the ST is a better choice. If you want to do the most sophisticated work, the Mac is the best bet. If you want to do hard-disk recording, you can go with a Mac, PC, or ST, though the Mac and PC offer more room to grow. If you're a bit more adventurous and like living on the edge, pop for an IRIS Indigo (hard-disk recording capability is built in, and MIDI sequencing software is available).

If you'll be doing non-musical work, consider that as well. Nothing can touch the Amiga and Video Toaster for video work, while the Mac excels at desktop publishing and other graphics applications and PCs offer a wealth of specialized business software.

In any event, you'll be spending a lot of time in front of the computer, so find something you can look at, work on, and live with for some time. You'll probably never regret purchasing more computer than you need, so don't worry about over-buying. Just have fun, and keep telling yourself, "Hey, it's a necessity." ♪

Sound Cards and MIDI Interfaces for the IBM PC

BY
DAVID (RUDY) TRUBITT

For many, the first step into the world of computer music involves a "sound card," such as the Sound Blaster. A sound card adds a great deal of sound-generating capability to a standard PC, allowing you to play back complete pieces of music with melodies, chords and drum accompaniment. Many sound cards also let you record your own sounds using digital-sampling technology (see "Unveiling the Mystery," p. 11). Best of all, sound cards for the PC are plentiful and relatively inexpensive, making them an excellent introduction to the world of computer music.

Sound cards offer a self-contained approach to music-making, but the real power of modern computer-music technology is the ability to expand your system to meet your unique needs. Perhaps you want to play music into your computer from a piano-style keyboard, or experiment with more exciting drum sounds than your sound card can create on its own. MIDI goes beyond the limitations of a single product by letting you create your own system from a number of individual pieces.

But in order for your PC to enter the world of MIDI, you'll need to equip it with a MIDI interface. This interface will add MIDI In and Out ports to your computer, allowing it to communicate with and control the rest of your MIDI gear. Many sound cards do have MIDI capabilities, although an external cable and connector box is usually required. Happily, there is a growing amount of educational and home-oriented software available to exploit the MIDI potential of popular sound cards.

However, if you want access to the many professional-grade MIDI software programs available for the PC, you should consider a more professional MIDI interface; though there is some support for sound card interfaces in the pro arena, it is limited. The interface you buy will have an impact on the software you'll be able to run, as MIDI interfaces and software programs are not automatically compatible. There is a *de facto* standard, Roland's MIDI Processing Unit (MPU-401), but its supremacy is slowly diminishing.

THE ROLAND MPU-401

When it was introduced in 1984, the principal selling point of the MPU-401 was the unit's Intelligent mode, which took care of many important MIDI tasks without bogging down the PC's central processor. The IBM PCs of 1984 had less power than today's models, so the MPU's processing capabilities were useful. Roland offered the MPU-401 chips to other companies, making it

Roland's SCC-1 combines an MPU-401 compatible MIDI interface with a 24-voice, multitimbral sound generator.

easy for them to make compatible products of their own. Enough MPU-style interfaces were sold that nearly every software company had to support the standard to stay competitive. This is still the case, as even programs designed specifically for non-MPU interfaces usually offer MPU-compatible versions.

The MPU-401's biggest advantage today is software compatibility. If you want to run the largest number of programs, especially shareware, you should still be looking at an MPU-compatible interface.

However, today's typical PC-compatible has increased in power to the point that it doesn't need the boost Intelligent mode offers. Also, Roland's MPU-401 chips discard MIDI Time Code (MTC) messages (see "The Secrets of Synchronization," p. 98) when in Intelligent mode. MIDI Time Code is important for many multitrack tape, hard-disk recording, and multimedia applications (see p. 101 for more info). As an alternative, the MPU can operate in Dumb mode (also called UART mode), which does pass MTC messages. In this case, the computer is responsible for everything and all features of Intelligent mode are lost. Many developers who support the MPU-401 today are using Dumb mode, despite the extra programming work it entails.

Several manufacturers have taken the basic MPU-401 and added additional MIDI ports (which help organize and improve the efficiency of very large MIDI systems) and SMPTE read/write capability, which allows your computer to run in sync with audio or video recorders (see "The Secrets of Synchronization," p. 98, for more on SMPTE). These interfaces function like an MPU-401 unless software is specifically written or updated to support the additional features. Check with manufacturers to find out if their software supports any "extras" that your interface provides.

MPU-401-compatible interfaces must be installed in an expansion slot, forcing laptop users to seek alternatives. Many

"IRQS: NINETY PERCENT OF THE PROBLEM"

*I*f you're having a problem installing a MIDI interface in your PC, your interface and some other plug-in card may both be trying to use the same *interrupt request line*, or IRQ.

IRQs are a way for parts of your PC system (such as a MIDI interface) to tell the CPU to stop what it's doing and take care of something that can't wait (such as reading incoming MIDI messages). This request is made by toggling the logic level of a pin on the expansion bus. If two cards are trying to toggle the same pin, the CPU may lock up.

MPU-401 interfaces normally are set to use IRQ2 when shipped. Other plug-in devices also may be set to IRQ2, and some Leading Edge and Tandy 1000s use IRQ2 for disk control or other functions. If the offending card cannot be removed to have its IRQ number changed, you'll have to change the IRQ settings on the MIDI interface. Most newer interfaces have user-selectable IRQs, but your software must be able to use the alternate IRQ or it won't recognize the presence of the interface. New programs generally offer this ability, but older programs and shareware may not be able to accommodate the alternate choice.

laptops use a MIDI interface that fits into the printer port; these can be either serial or parallel. You'll have to call your software vendor to find out if their programs support these interfaces, as none of the serial or parallel interfaces are MPU-compatible.

BUILT-IN SOUND AND PREPACKAGED SYSTEMS

Several manufacturers make cards that incorporate MIDI interfaces with onboard synthesizers, which are well-suited for educational applications. Game software also can take advantage of this type of device for generating sound effects and music that are synchronized with the onscreen action.

Some systems of this type, such as the SoundBlaster, are not MPU-compatible and require an external connector box to access their MIDI interface functions. In some cases, the MIDI implementation of game-oriented boards may be limited, so read the fine print.

Many MIDI interfaces contain some kind of tape-sync capability, but nearly all the signals they put on tape (with the exception of SMPTE) are incompatible with each other.

WHO'S DRIVING THIS THING ANYWAY?

But why aren't all interfaces compatible with all MIDI software? To transmit and receive MIDI messages, a special software program called a *device driver* is required. The application program communicates with the driver program, rather than with the interface itself. Typically, a device driver is designed into each application program and, sadly, different programs' drivers are incompatible.

To achieve the blissful state of *device independence,* in which the user can select software and hardware without concern for

compatibility, a system-wide driver must be written to support a number of interfaces, and programmers must agree to support the protocols used by that driver. Such a driver can also be designed to manage access from several programs simultaneously in a multitasking environment, such as Microsoft's *Windows* (see "Multimedia Windows for the PC," p. 113). Currently, every PC MIDI interface manufacturer who offers a non-MPU-401 compatible interface already provides or is working on a *Windows* driver.

In summary, let your software requirements drive your hardware purchase. If you aren't sure of your future needs, an MPU-401-compatible interface is still a safe choice, but if you're only planning to run *Windows* MIDI programs it's not a necessity. If you are primarily putting together a system to run one package, ask the software vendor for a hardware recommendation. ♪

Music Quest's MQX-16 combines MPU-401 compatibility and sophisticated tape synchronization capabilities on a compact plug-in card.

MIDI Manager
for the Macintosh

I f you use MIDI software on the Macintosh, you've probably at least heard of Apple's *MIDI Manager,* and you may already own *MIDI Manager*-compatible applications. Let's take a look at *MIDI Manager*'s good and bad points, and why it exists.

While *MultiFinder* made it possible to run several programs at once, it was of limited use for MIDI applications until *MIDI Manager* arrived. For instance, put your non-*MIDI Manager* sequencer into play, then try to switch to another application without stopping it. Can't do it, can you?

There's a reason for this: To maintain accuracy, MIDI programs traditionally have taken over the Mac's hardware, communicating with its serial ports directly and setting up its timer for their own use. If another application tries to make use of the timer or the serial ports while a sequencer is playing, there will be problems and possibly even a system crash.

Most non-*MIDI Manager* programs politely reconfigure the hardware and reinstall their drivers when they are switched off under *MultiFinder* or System 7. If you are running a patch editor and a sequencer, each program will disconnect itself when switched to the background and reconnect when brought to the front. This is better

than having to quit one application to run another, but it falls far short of realizing multitasking's full potential. Multitasking is impossible because neither application can send or receive MIDI messages while the other is active.

ENTER MIDI MANAGER

To work together, MIDI applications needed to get away from the direct hardware connection. Instead of each application having its own *driver* (a low-level routine that talks directly to the Macintosh serial ports and timers), developers needed a single, system-level driver that could be shared by multiple MIDI applications. Apple created *MIDI Manager* to address this need.

Besides letting multiple MIDI applications send and receive on the modem and printer ports, *MIDI Manager* lets you connect the output of one application directly to the input of another for real-time data sharing. For example, you could send MIDI data generated by an algorithmic composition program directly to a sequencer or notation program. A program called *PatchBay* lets you make these input, output, and timing connections graphically by dragging "patch cords" to connect *MIDI Manager* ports (see **Fig. 1.12**).

BY
NIGEL
REDMON

25

MIDI Manager for the Macintosh

WHAT MIDI MANAGER BRINGS TO THE PARTY

Products such as Digidesign's Sample Cell (a sample playback card that fits inside your Mac) would be impractical without *MIDI Manager*. With it, application programs can send Note On messages to a Sample Cell card directly, without a MIDI interface or cables.

MIDI Manager opens many possibilities for software as well. For instance, a MIDI processing application could be connected between the output of a sequencer and the MIDI interface to add arpeggiation, note mapping, or other real-time effects.

Another benefit of *MIDI Manager* is that it isolates MIDI applications from the hardware. If Apple introduces a new computer, it only has to update *MIDI Manager* and the other system software. All your *MIDI Manager* applications are automatically compatible. If someone designs a new interface, they only have to write a driver to work with all *MIDI Manager* applications.

MIDI Manager doesn't do anything for applications that don't know about it. In the absence of *MIDI Manager*, MIDI applications will use their direct MIDI drivers. Older applications must be updated by the manufacturer to work with *MIDI Manager* and, thankfully, most have been. New programs are generally being written to work with it from the start. Some of them, such as Opcode's *Max* and EarLevel Engineering's *HyperMIDI 2.0*, take advantage of *MIDI Manager's* capabilities by allowing up to six input ports and six output ports.

THE PRICE YOU PAY

When it's running, *MIDI Manager* is busy behind the scenes, managing data and time to keep all of its clients happy. This means virtually all of your interaction with your Mac will be slower. This effect will be especially noticeable if you are accustomed to a particular application and then start using it under *MIDI Manager*.

However, *MIDI Manager* is only active when a compatible application is running. It occupies little memory, and its overhead will not affect performance if you are not running a *MIDI Manager* application. Furthermore, its overhead will not affect your MIDI timing. In fact, the major reason for the slowdown is that *MIDI Manager* gives absolute priority to timing in order to ensure accurate recording and playback.

Is it worth the overhead to use *MIDI Manager*? On the faster Macs, the answer for most people will be "yes." If you want to use NuBus-based MIDI devices such as Mac-Proteus or Sample Cell, you must use *MIDI Manager* or Opcode's *OMS* (see p. 27).

On the slower Macintoshes—the Plus, SE, and Classic—you'll have to make the call yourself. Complex MIDI applications with frequent screen updating and many data-manipulation options already run slowly on these machines. The added load could push you over the edge and diminish your productivity and fun.

If you do use *MIDI Manager*, be sure you have the latest version. Better performance, fewer serious bugs, and compatibility with all Macintosh models make it a worthwhile upgrade.

MIDI Manager is an achievement in many ways, not the least of which is Apple's acknowledgment of the computer musician's needs. With computers getting faster and the MIDI musician's options constantly increasing, the future can only get better. ♪

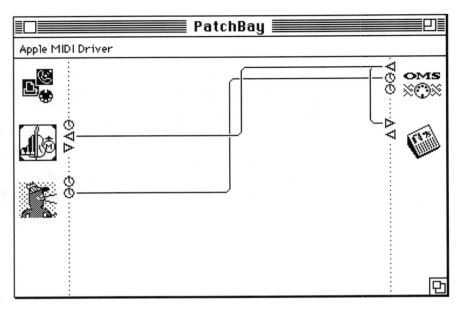

Figure 1.12 The *PatchBay* window with several MIDI applications running. The Apple MIDI Driver icon appears in the upper left corner, with the modem port enabled. Notice that you can connect several outputs to a single input; the input will merge the incoming MIDI data. Also, an output can connect to more than one input.

The Opcode MIDI System (OMS)

A s computer-based MIDI systems grow more and more complex, the need for effective management systems for them increases accordingly. MIDI software developer Opcode recognized this need and developed a System Extension (or INIT) for the Macintosh called the *Opcode MIDI System (OMS)*. *OMS* provides integrated control over the various aspects of a MIDI studio while coordinating the activities of different Opcode applications and reducing the need to enter system details (such as MIDI channels) more than once.

At the most basic level, *OMS* functions as a device driver. In this role, *OMS* allows compatible applications to use a variety of Mac MIDI interfaces, including Mark Of The Unicorn's MIDI Time Piece and Opcode's Studio 5. *OMS* also complements Apple's *MIDI Manager* without replacing it. (see "MIDI Manager for the Macintosh," p. 25).

OMS also provides a central location for storing the details of your entire MIDI system. Best of all, Opcode currently includes *OMS* free with most of its software. With that in mind, let's take it from the top.

WHY OMS?

Opcode set out to address a number of problems with *OMS*. First, the increasing size of professional MIDI systems was getting out of hand. *OMS* was designed to provide centralized control for large MIDI systems. Another goal in the development of *OMS* was to reduce any duplication of effort by users. For example, in its pre-*OMS* incarnation, Opcode's universal librarian program, *Galaxy,* required you to define MIDI receive channels, device ID numbers, and so on. Much of this information also was useful for the company's *Vision* sequencer, but each required separate entry of the same information. *OMS* solves this problem by providing a single repository for the system description. The information is entered once, and if changed, is automatically updated everywhere it is used.

OMS AND MIDI MANAGER

Before *OMS*, the only way to access plug-in Mac cards such as Sample Cell and MacProteus was by way of Apple's *MIDI Manager.* Unfortunately, early users who tried to use Sample Cell while running *Studio Vision* found that only a Mac IIci or IIfx

BY
DAVID (RUDY)
TRUBITT

had the horsepower to run both applications along with *MIDI Manager*. Because *OMS* requires less computer power than *MIDI Manager, Studio Vision* and Sample Cell now can run together with *OMS* on slower Mac IIs.

This situation might lead to some confusion about the purpose of *OMS* vis-a-vis *MIDI Manager. OMS* was not designed to replace *MIDI Manager*, the programs can be used together or separately. However, users who need both find the combination to be cumbersome at times. The biggest difference between *OMS* and *MIDI Manager* is that the latter supports inter-application communication (IAC), while *OMS* does not. For the few cases in which two MIDI programs must run synchronously, *MIDI Manager* is the only answer.

SETTING UP

To configure *OMS*, you actually describe your entire MIDI system graphically. **Fig. 1.13** illustrates the setup window in which this description is specified.

As you might guess, black arrows represent MIDI connections, and gray arrows represent unconnected ports. Fortunately, *OMS* is well-equipped to deal with multiport interfaces and MIDI patch bays, such as the DMC MX-8 depicted in **Fig. 1.13**. Although things look a bit complicated at first glance, it's really not that difficult to get up and running. *OMS* even provides a handy test mode which makes it easy to see if everything's really hooked up the way you think it is.

In addition to displaying information graphically, a dialog box such as the one in **Fig. 1.14** can be opened by double-clicking on a device in the *OMS* setup window. This is where you define specific information about the individual devices in your setup. Is the device multitimbral? On what channel(s) will it receive data? In this case, I disabled channels 13 to 16 on my Proteus, which is indicated by the missing X's in **Fig. 1.14**. The sync options identify the elements in the system that send or receive MIDI Clock messages.

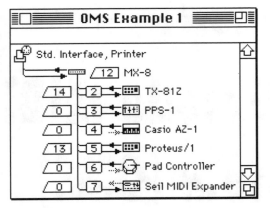

Figure 1.13 The OMS Setup window graphically depicts your MIDI system. In this example, an MX-8 MIDI patch bay is connected to a standard MIDI interface in the Mac's printer port.

If your MIDI patch bay can respond to Program Change messages, *OMS* allows *Galaxy* to switch patch bay configurations as needed. It's extremely convenient to hop out of *Vision*, pull a patch bank from a synth, edit a patch, and return to the sequencer without pushing buttons on your MIDI patch bay. When *Galaxy* needs patch data from a device, it looks up the appropriate patch bay configuration and makes the switch automatically. As soon as the data is transferred, *OMS* returns the patch bay to the default configuration.

OMS AND THE STUDIO 5

A special version of *OMS* is shipped with every Studio 5 (see **Fig. 1.15**, p. 31). It includes all of the features mentioned so far, plus three more: *virtual controllers, virtual instruments,* and *patches.*

Figure 1.14 Double-clicking on a device in the Setup window opens a dialog box in which you specify additional information about that device.

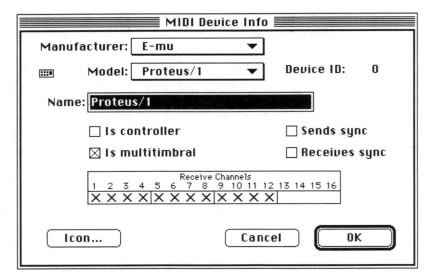

A *virtual controller* is used to process the MIDI output of a MIDI controller. A number of processing options exist, but the most common ones are MIDI data filtering, thinning, and scaling. Virtual controllers are defined in their own *OMS* window and use the computing power of the Studio 5 to perform their tasks. This setup allows you to modify data before it gets to your sequencer, rather than editing it after recording.

Virtual instruments integrate MIDI sound modules with MIDI data processing. In effect, they complement the virtual controllers by processing the data from a sequencer before it reaches a sound module. The basic processing options for virtual instruments allow you to split and layer sound modules, although they also include a range of continuous-controller scaling and processing options.

Finally, *patches* are combinations of virtual instruments and controllers along with overall MIDI routing, merging, additional MIDI processing, Program Change assignments, and other features. The combination of *OMS's* MIDI processing power and the Studio 5's large number of MIDI inputs and outputs makes for a very sophisticated yet surprisingly easy-to-use MIDI system.

OMS AND THE MARKETPLACE

Opcode hopes that the *OMS* system will be adopted by other software developers, and many have indeed agreed to do so. Other companies are interested as well, but support from all parties is far from guaranteed. As you might expect, technical, marketing, and customer considerations pull in different directions, and only time will tell where the *OMS* path will lead. Nevertheless, the program is a big step toward taming those ever-expanding MIDI systems, and it offers immediate benefits to users of Opcode software. ♪

Multi-Port MIDI

BY DAVID (RUDY) TRUBITT

Here's a troubling observation: Everything will be stretched to the limit sooner than anyone dreamed possible. Take MIDI's sixteen channels, which once seemed like *soooo* many. But what's the problem? Can't more channels just be added to the MIDI spec? To explain why it's not so simple, let's take a brief trip to the land of (suspenseful music...) *binary arithmetic!* (Shriek! Slam!)

When the MIDI messages were defined, four binary bits were set aside for the channel number. It turns out that there are exactly sixteen unique combinations of these four bits. Thus, adding more channels would require more bits. Unfortunately, adding even one extra bit to any standard MIDI message would confuse every piece of MIDI equipment around today. So what else can be done? I thought you'd never ask. Let's talk about (drum roll...) *multi-port MIDI interfaces!* (Wild applause.)

Basic MIDI interfaces have one input and output "port." In contrast, multi-port interfaces have more than one MIDI out and often have extra MIDI ins. These additional ins and outs can each carry a full load of unique data; in other words, their own set of sixteen MIDI channels. This extra MIDI capacity can improve the performance and convenience of your system. However, multi-ports are more expensive than basic MIDI interfaces, and are best suited for large, multi-device MIDI systems.

Note that while many basic interfaces provide multiple convenience outputs, identical data is sent from each. Don't mistake these devices for multi-port interfaces; what we are talking about is *independently addressable* MIDI ins and outs.

THE BENEFITS

Some of the most important benefits of multi-port interfaces are:

• **More Channels** Sixteen channels are enough for many uses, but even modest setups can stretch that limit, especially if you use MIDI to control effects units or other non-synthesizer equipment.

• **Higher Speeds** Although each independent port's cable carries data at the standard 31.25 kHz rate, two cables have twice the capacity of one. This can help prevent "MIDI logjams," which occur if your computer sends data faster than MIDI can carry it, or (more commonly) faster than receiving equipment can process it. Logjams cause timing inaccuracies and lost data. This isn't a problem for everyone; it's most likely if you're using lots of continuous controllers, working with dense music, or synching to MIDI time code. Remember that there will *always* be a bottleneck somewhere. Adding a multi-port interface might reveal that your computer was barely fast enough to keep up with your old interface.

Figure 1.15 Highlights of Opcode's Studio 5 MIDI interface for the Mac include 15 independent MIDI ins and outs and tape sync. The Studio 5 makes extensive use of OMS (see previous chapter).

• **Greater Integration** An interface with enough ins and outs can eliminate the need for a MIDI patch bay. This helps keep your MIDI routing in one place under your computer's control, rather than spread out between different boxes. Some interfaces, including Mark of the Unicorn's MIDI Time Piece (see **Fig. 1.16**) and MIDI Time Piece II, and Opcode's Studio 4 and Studio 5 (see **Fig. 1.15**), can act as comprehensive MIDI control centers, routing data from any input to any output and performing merging, filtering, and rechannelization.

Many of these interfaces also include SMPTE or other tape sync capability. Besides the advantage of fewer little boxes, putting SMPTE on the interface has additional benefits. Placing the interface under computer control saves you from worrying about frame rates, etc.; your software should take care of it. It also means that sync information is kept off your MIDI cables, reducing logjam potential.

• **Smaller Headaches** Finally, multiple MIDI outs make it easier to work with both high- and low-end equipment. For example, most inexpensive home keyboards are MIDI-compatible, but some have fixed channel assignments. This can be inconvenient, especially if you have two instruments stuck on the same channel. At the other extreme, some instruments receive notes on all sixteen channels at once, requiring you to disable channels used by other instruments. In both cases, dedicating a separate MIDI line to each of these instruments lets you concentrate on music, rather than channel assignments.

COMPATIBILITY

The question of compatibility is a particularly important one. Unless software vendors specifically support the interface, the extra in and out ports can't be used. In some cases, one company's interface is unusable by any other company's software. As always, it's up to you to verify the compatibility of your computer purchases. IBM users are reminded to consider the benefits of MPU-401 compatibility (see "Sound Cards and MIDI Interfaces for the IBM PC," p. 22).

All Atari ST interfaces are made by companies which also provide software. You're probably best off buying your software and interface from the same company. Note that ST multi-ports allow you to use the ST's built-in MIDI interface as well. This adds one to the number of ins and outs provided by your multi-port interface itself.

On the Macintosh, things are a little simpler. Basic one-in, one-out MIDI interfaces work with any MIDI program, and many programs can operate with two basic interfaces hooked up to the same computer. As far as Mac multi-port interfaces are concerned, a quick call to the developer of the software you plan to use is recommended. ♪

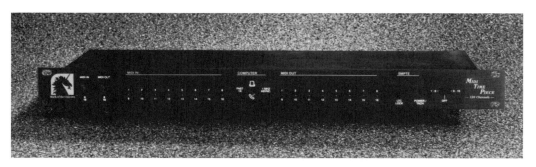

Figure 1.16 Mark of the Unicorn's MIDI Time Piece offers 8 individual MIDI ins and outs and tape synchronization capability. Although originally designed for the Mac, a plug-in card for PC compatibles enables the MTP to work with several PC sequencer programs as well.

2

Recording Your Music

Understanding Sequencing

I f you're excited by the potential benefits of MIDI and electronic music but unfamiliar with the nuts and bolts (or chips and software) that make them work, you're not alone. Perhaps you've read something about sequencing or watched someone do it, but still don't understand the details of the process. Even if you own a MIDI keyboard and sequencer, you may be unable to learn sequencing fundamentals from their owner's manuals (which isn't surprising, since most manuals are incomprehensible even to seasoned veterans).

If this describes your situation, read on. As you'll see, sequencing isn't that difficult, once you get the hang of it.

TAPE DECKS VS. SEQUENCERS

Conceptually, sequencing is similar to multitrack tape recording, where individual musical parts are stored on their own tape tracks and can be accessed independently for recording, editing and mixing. In fact, sequencers can be thought of as MIDI recorders. (To comprehend the principles of sequencing, it helps to have a basic understanding of MIDI itself; see "What Is MIDI?" on p. 7.)

In the sequencing process, you play a keyboard or other MIDI instrument and your performance is recorded into the sequencer. After recording, you can play back your performance and listen or record additional parts. However, unlike a tape recorder, the sequencer does *not* record the actual sounds that you produce on the instrument.

This point is so important, it deserves an example. Let's say you play a MIDI keyboard and record your performance with a sequencer. As you record, the patch on the keyboard is a string sound. After recording, you change the patch on the keyboard to a flute sound and play the sequence back. The part you just recorded is played back faithfully, but with the flute sound instead of the string sound.

This occurs because sequencers record the MIDI messages that are sent from the instrument as you play, such as Note On, Note Off, Pitch Bend, Aftertouch, Sustain Pedal, and so on. In our example, the sequencer simply recorded the note messages you played. (If you want, you could have the sequencer record a Program Change message, which would reset the synthesizer to the sound of your choice.)

The messages generated by a MIDI instrument are carried along a MIDI cable from the instrument to the sequencer, which is nothing more than a computer dedicated to the task of recording, storing, and manipulating a *sequence*, or list, of MIDI messages (hence the name "sequencer").

BY
**SCOTT
WILKINSON**

When you play back the recording, the sequencer sends the MIDI messages back to the instrument, which responds by playing the part as if you were playing the instrument directly.

SIMILARITIES AND DIFFERENCES

The conceptual similarity between sequencers and tape decks can be seen in the main controls found on most sequencers, which are Play, Record, Stop, Pause, Fast Forward, and Rewind. Also, almost all sequencers have more than one track, allowing you to record new parts while listening to ones you recorded previously.

However, the differences between a sequencer and a tape deck outnumber the similarities. As stated before, sequencers do not record sound at all. Also, the "transport" is instantaneous; unlike on a tape deck, pressing the Rewind button on a sequencer takes you to the beginning of a song instantly. Many sequencers have more tracks than the most expensive tape decks (sometimes hundreds). In addition, sequencers allow you to slow down and speed up the tempo of a song while recording or playing back without affecting the pitch of the music. This can be handy if you only can play certain passages slowly; simply record at a slower tempo and speed it up for playback.

The primary advantage of sequencers is their editing capabilities. Compared to magnetic tape, editing on a sequencer is far easier and more precise and comprehensive. Many people claim that sequencers offer the same advantages over tape decks that word processors offer over typewriters, which is true in many respects. Although sequencers can't manipulate sound directly, they can manipulate the MIDI messages in an entire performance, one track, or even a single note with a variety of editing techniques, such as cut-and-paste and transposition.

On a tape deck, the "memory" is a reel of tape. The length of the tape determines the maximum length of the material that can be recorded. On a sequencer, the memory is RAM (Random Access Memory), which also determines the length of the material that can be recorded. Unlike tape, the capacity of which is measured in minutes, sequencer memory is measured by the number of events or notes that it can accommodate, regardless of their length. When comparing the capacity of different sequencers, it's important to remember that a "note" consists of two MIDI events: Note On and Note Off. If the capacity of a sequencer is specified as a number of events, the note capacity probably is half that amount.

Another distinction between tape decks and sequencers concerns the difference between tracks and MIDI channels. As you might already know, most MIDI messages are sent on one of sixteen channels, each of which can accommodate up to sixteen notes of polyphony. This means that up to sixteen independent polyphonic parts can be carried on one MIDI cable.

A track on a tape deck usually holds only one musical part, unless you "bounce" (mix and re-record) several recorded tracks onto a single track. However, a track in a sequencer can include parts on any or all of the sixteen MIDI channels, which means that up to sixteen different parts can occupy a single track. Essentially, each track in a sequencer provides sixteen "virtual tracks" that correspond to the sixteen MIDI channels. (Typically, each musical part in a sequence is played on its own separate MIDI channel.)

A sequencer also lets you bounce parts on one channel or track to other tracks. When you bounce parts from one track to another on a tape deck, you lose some sound quality in the process. But with a sequencer, the sound quality never degrades, because the sound actually comes from the instrument itself as it is played by the sequencer.

EQUIPMENT

Now that some of the basic concepts are out of the way, it's time to deal with equipment requirements for MIDI sequencing. First in the chain is some sort of MIDI controller, such as a keyboard, MIDI guitar, MIDI wind controller, or MIDI drum pads. This is the device that you actually play, sending MIDI messages to the sequencer.

Next in line is the sequencer itself, which comes in one of several forms: stand-alone hardware, integrated hardware, or software. Stand-alone hardware sequencers are generally small and portable, making them good for gigs and tours. However, they often have small displays and are not easily updated with new features. Also, less expensive models might not even have a floppy disk drive for permanent storage.

Integrated hardware sequencers are built into keyboard *workstations*. They function identically to stand-alone sequencers, but don't require a physical MIDI connection between the keyboard and sequencer; all communications are handled internally.

Software sequencers are programs written for common general-purpose computers such as the Apple Macintosh, Atari ST, Commodore Amiga, or IBM PC and compatibles. These sequencers offer a larger display (the computer screen), easily installed updates, permanent disk storage, and more sophisticated features. Of course, they are usually less portable than hardware sequencers (unless you are fortunate enough to own a laptop computer with a MIDI interface).

All sequencers, regardless of type, can be divided into two basic categories (although many include aspects of both): *linear* and *pattern-oriented*. Linear sequencers provide the closest analogy to tape decks, with several tracks on which you record different parts from the beginning of the song to the end. Pattern-oriented sequencers follow a drum-machine analogy: You record short patterns that later are strung together to form a whole song.

At the other end of the sequencing chain, you need some sort of MIDI sound module that will respond to the MIDI messages sent from the sequencer. This sound module might be incorporated into the keyboard or other MIDI instrument controller, or it could be an external unit. In either case, the most cost-effective type of sound module is one that is *multitimbral*, meaning that it can play several parts with different sounds on different MIDI channels at the same time. It often takes only one such sound module to play an entire song.

Whether you use a workstation or separate units, you also need a sound system of some sort to hear what you're doing. This might be a simple pair of headphones or a *mixer* with an amplifier and a pair of speakers.

Fig. 2.1 provides an example of a typical MIDI sequencing system. The keyboard includes its own single-timbre

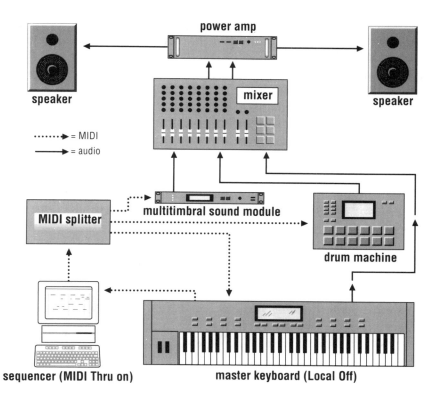

sound module, which is set to receive on MIDI channel 1. The external sound module is multitimbral, capable of producing up to eight different sounds on channels 2 to 9. The other elements of the system include a drum machine (set to receive on channel 10), the sequencer itself, and a sound system. As you can see, the MIDI Out from the keyboard is connected to the MIDI In of the sequencer, and the MIDI Out from the sequencer is connected to the MIDI Ins of the keyboard, sound module, and drum machine using a MIDI splitter, or MIDI Thru box. You also could connect the MIDI Thru of each device into the MIDI In of the next.

Most sequencers have a function called "Thru" or "Echo" that regulates whether or not the incoming MIDI messages will be sent right back out in addition to being recorded. Turning on this function allows you to hear an external sound module or drum machine respond as you play on the keyboard and record into the sequencer. The MIDI messages are sent from the keyboard into the sequencer and on to the sound module.

However, if you play the keyboard's own sound generator from the keyboard while the sequencer's Thru function is on, MIDI messages will be sent from the instrument to the sequencer and right back to the instrument again. At best, this will

Figure 2.1 A complete computer sequencing system. Note how MIDI connections center around the computer while audio cables lead to the mixer and on to the amp and speakers. Both audio and MIDI connections are a necessary part of any sequencing setup.

result in each note being played twice—once by you and once by the sequencer, as the MIDI messages are reflected back to the instrument—which will cut the polyphony of the instrument in half. At worst, the result will be stuck notes (notes that don't turn off) and other weirdnesses associated with MIDI feedback loops.

To avoid these problems, you can turn the sequencer's Thru function off when recording the keyboard's own part. However, it often is preferable to turn off the keyboard's "Local Mode" instead. This prevents the keyboard from triggering its own sound generator, but doesn't interfere with the MIDI messages it generates. You can play on the keyboard and record parts for the external sound module while the sequencer plays the sound-generating circuitry built into the keyboard.

RECORDING & PLAYBACK

The two basic types of sequence recording are real-time and step-time. *Real-time sequencing* resembles audio tape recording: after some preliminary setup, simply press Record and play the desired part.

All sequencers provide some sort of *metronome* for real-time sequencing. The metronome establishes the tempo and provides a reference for your performance. The sound of the metronome might be generated within the sequencer itself as a click, or it might be sent at regular intervals from the sequencer as a MIDI Note On message on one of the MIDI channels. This message is meant to be played by an external sound module, typically a drum machine set to something like a rim-shot sound. Most devices and programs let you specify a *count-in*, in which the metronome plays for a number of bars before the sequencer starts recording. This lets you get a sense of the tempo before you start playing.

If the song you want to sequence is too difficult for you to play at the intended tempo, you can slow down the metronome until you can play it easily. If you tried to do this with a tape recorder, the performance would sound much higher in pitch when you played it back at the right speed. However, a sequencer can change the speed of playback without changing the pitch, because it records a sequence of MIDI messages rather than actual sounds.

The messages specify the pitch of the notes, while the sequencer controls how quickly they are sent to the instrument that's playing them.

Once you've recorded one part, you can record additional parts in a process called *overdubbing*. The sequencer will play the part you previously recorded while recording the new part. If your sequencer has many tracks, it is a good idea to record the different drum and percussion parts (kick, snare, hi-hat, etc.) on separate tracks so that you can edit them separately.

Returning to **Fig. 2.1**, let's say that the keyboard's internal sound module is set to play a piano sound on MIDI channel 1. (Remember to turn the keyboard's Local function off and the sequencer's Thru function on.) The multitimbral sound module should be set to play a bass sound on channel 2, a rhythm guitar sound on channel 3, a lead synth sound on channel 4, a punchy horn sound on channel 5, and an additional bass sound on channel 6. The drum machine will play the drum part on channel 10. For now, the drum machine acts like a passive sound module, producing drum sounds without using its internal drum-programming capabilities. Its part will be recorded into the sequencer along with all the other parts. The following procedure illustrates the basic recording process.

PROCEDURE: REAL-TIME RECORDING

1. On the sequencer, select real-time recording and set a tempo at which you wish to record your song. Remember that, if necessary, you can set a slower tempo than the song requires.

2. Set the count-in so that you know when to start. A typical count-in is two bars long.

3. Decide which part you want to record first. Many people record the drum part first so that they have a sense of the "groove" when recording the other parts. Others prefer to record the piano part first to get a sense of the whole song. You might want to record a condensed piano version of the whole song even if such a part won't be in the final recording. You can play subsequent parts to this piano reference and delete it later.

4. On the keyboard, set the MIDI transmit channel to match the instrument you've selected. If it's the piano part, set the controller to transmit on MIDI channel 1; if it's the drum part, set it to channel 10.

5. Play a few notes on the keyboard to ensure the MIDI messages are getting to the right sound module.

6. On the sequencer, select the track on which you wish to record the part, enable its Record function, and press Record.

7. After the count-in, perform the selected instrument's part in time with the metronome.

8. After recording, press Stop.

9. Press Rewind and disable the track's Record function.

10. Press Play to hear the new part.

11. To overdub the next part, press Stop and Rewind. Select the next part to record and repeat steps 4 through 9 until all parts are recorded.

Step-time sequencing differs from real-time sequencing in that the notes or chords of each part are recorded one at a time without playing to a metronome. This allows you to record parts that are impossible to play otherwise. However, it also results in a very machine-like recording. Step-time sequencing is a tedious job, but it provides a means to record musical ideas that are too difficult to play in real time.

PROCEDURE: STEP-TIME RECORDING

1. Select the part you wish to record and set the keyboard's transmit channel accordingly.

2. On the sequencer, select step-time recording, select the track on which you wish to record, enable its Record function, and press Record.

3. On the sequencer, select the duration value (whole note, eighth-note triplet, etc.) for the first note or chord.

4. On the keyboard, play the first note or chord. You needn't play any particular rhythm or duration; the sequencer simply records the note or chord you play and assigns the specified duration to it.

5. On the sequencer, select the duration value for the next note or chord and play it on the keyboard.

6. Repeat step 5 until the entire part is recorded.

7. On the sequencer, press Rewind and disable the track's Record function.

8. Press Play if you want to hear the part you just recorded. You might have to exit step-time mode and adjust the tempo setting.

9. Select the next part to record and follow steps 1 through 8. Repeat these steps until all parts are recorded.

EDITING

One of the main advantages of the sequencer over the tape recorder is editing. If you make a few mistakes, most sequencers have many types of editing functions which allow you to fix them. These functions can be applied to an entire song, sections of a song (such as the chorus), individual tracks, sections of tracks (such as bars 9 to 16), MIDI channels, specific note ranges (such as C4 to B4), types of events (such as *MIDI Volume* messages), or even single events (such as one note). Typically, you simply select the event, section, or type of message you want to edit and apply the desired editing function.

For example, you can transpose the notes in any specified range up or down by a number of semitones. The events in the specified range can be *channelized* to a different MIDI channel and shifted forward or backward in small increments of time, which changes the feel of the part. The specified range of events also can be merged with other events, which is useful for combining tracks in a manner similar to "bouncing" tape tracks. This also means that messages on different MIDI channels can coexist on a single track.

One of the most important editing functions is *quantization*, which allows you to clean up sloppy rhythms in a variety of ways. Basically, quantization shifts each selected event to coincide with a user-specified rhythmic position. It's usually applied to notes, but it can be applied to other MIDI messages in some sequencers.

For example, let's say you apply quarter-note quantization to all the notes in a particular track. If a note starts right on a quarter-note position (beat 1, 2, 3, etc.), it is left alone. However, if the note starts slightly ahead of a quarter-note position, it is shifted back to coincide with that position. Similarly, a note that starts a bit late is shifted forward. This helps clean up slightly sloppy playing, but notes that are far off the mark might get shifted to an unintended position (see **Fig. 2.2**).

When used, quantization almost always is applied to Note On events. It also can be applied to Note Off events, although this may change the duration of the notes, and the result sounds like it was entered in step time. Most sequencers offer the option to preserve the performed duration of quantized notes by shifting Note Off events by the same amount as the Note On events.

In general, you should use a quantization value equal to the shortest note in the section to be quantized. If you have alternating triplet and duplet figures, you should quantize each figure separately. This is a real drag, but quantizing eighth-note triplets into straight eighth notes destroys the triplets.

It's important to recognize when and where quantization should and shouldn't be applied. If you quantize everything, your music will sound mechanical and uninteresting (unless the style of music you're playing calls for very precise rhythmic accuracy). My preference is to quantize as little as possible, but there are situations in which it helps the overall sound. For example, the kick drum and bass parts should be dead-on together, especially on the downbeats, so it might be a good idea to quantize these parts. On the other hand, a lead solo should not be quantized: The juxtaposition of a quantized rhythm section and fluid solo can be quite exciting.

Another important editing function available on most sequencers is *cut-and-paste*. As its name implies, this capability lets you cut or copy a section of a song or track and paste it elsewhere. For example, you can record a repeating background part only once and then copy and paste it throughout the song. This is not unlike the cut-and-paste function found in most word processors.

The events in a sequence also can be displayed in a variety of ways, providing a visual representation of the music and allowing you to select the events you wish to edit. Because of their small displays, hardware sequencers only offer an *event list* that presents the events in a list of numbers. This allows you to change a single note or other event such as a Program Change quite easily, but it's cumbersome if you're trying to change a stream of controller messages. Most hardware sequencers also offer the ability to select a specific type of event in a specific section of a song or track (or on a specific MIDI channel) for global editing functions such as transposition or quantization.

Software sequencers often include event-list editing, but they usually offer graphic editing as well. Thanks to a large computer screen, many events can be displayed at once. This display usually takes the form of a strip chart much like a piano roll (see **Fig. 2.2**), although some programs also have standard musical notation. A graphic editor also allows you to draw continuous Control Change messages such as Modulation Wheel on the screen with a mouse or other pointing device. In the case of programs that offer several different editing modes, it's important to remember that you're always working with the same musical information. The different modes simply provide different ways of looking at and working with the musical data.

In the following procedure, several basic editing functions are illustrated by specific examples. It assumes that several parts already have been recorded on several tracks. Although this procedure probably will not apply directly to your needs, it should give you an idea of how to edit your songs.

Figure 2.2 The graphic editing window from Opcode's *Vision* for the Macintosh. In this example, the C3 eighth notes are not quantized, while the F2 eighth notes were played with the same rhythm and quantized to quarter-note resolution. In both cases, all notes are supposed to start on consecutive beats. Notice that the first note was played a bit late and the second note was played a bit early, but both were shifted to their correct positions. The third note was played so late that it was shifted to beat four instead of beat three.

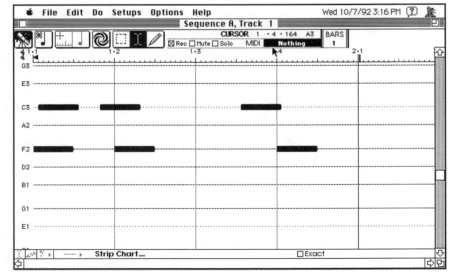

PROCEDURE: EDITING

1. To transpose the horn part up an octave, select the track on which the part was recorded (or select MIDI channel 5, according to the settings I specified earlier) and apply an upward transposition of twelve semitones.

2. To layer the bass part with the other bass sound (on channel 6) in the multitimbral sound module, select the bass track, copy it, and paste it to an empty track. Now select the new track and channelize it to channel 6.

3. To shift the snare-drum part slightly behind the beat, select the snare track and shift backward by several clock pulses. Listen to the result and adjust it until it sounds right.

4. To quantize the kick-drum and bass parts (assuming that the parts have no triplets and notes no shorter than sixteenths), select the appropriate tracks and apply sixteenth-note quantization. You might have to adjust some notes individually if they are too far from their intended positions.

5. Once the drum tracks are edited to your satisfaction, you can merge them together. Select one track as the final drum track and merge the other tracks into it. You might have to do this one track at a time.

6. To fix your solo lead line, which is perfect except for one wrong note, select the note and change its pitch to correct the error.

SYNCHRONIZATION

Previously, the drum machine has been used as a passive sound module and its parts have been recorded into the sequencer along with everything else. But what if you've already programmed some great patterns or songs into the drum machine and you want to use them as they are? Is there any way to synchronize the drum machine's performance with the sequencer so that the drum patterns play in time with the rest of the sequenced material?

Actually, it's relatively easy. In a process called *MIDI synchronization*, special MIDI messages are sent from the sequencer to coordinate the drum machine's performance (see "The Secrets of Synchronization," p. 98). This saves memory that could

be used to record the drum parts, which is important with small-capacity hardware sequencers. It also allows you to use the drum machine as a "groove" metronome, which is more inspiring than a click.

The special MIDI messages are called *real-time* messages. They include Start (which tells the drum machine to start playing from the beginning of the selected pattern or song), MIDI Clock (which is sent 24 times per quarter note and defines the tempo), Stop (which tells the drum machine to stop playing), and Continue (which tells the drum machine to start playing from the point at which it was stopped). Another real-time message is *Song Position Pointer*, which tells the drum machine where to start playing if you jump to another part of the song. Unfortunately, many drum machines do not respond to Song Position Pointer.

PROCEDURE: MIDI SYNCHRONIZATION

1. On the sequencer, set the sync mode to Master or Internal.

2. On the drum machine, set the sync mode to Slave, MIDI, or External.

3. On the drum machine, select the pattern or song you wish to play along with the sequencer. You can automate this on some machines by sending a Program Change message at the beginning of the sequence of events.

4. Press Play on the drum machine. It won't start playing; instead, it's put into a mode that waits for a Start message from the sequencer.

5. Press Play or Record on the sequencer. The drum machine will start playing in sync with the sequencer.

6. Press Stop on the sequencer. The drum machine will stop with the sequencer. Pressing Continue on the sequencer would start the two again from the stopping point.

While sequencing is invaluable for recording electronic instrumental parts, it can't handle vocals or acoustic instruments (there are several sequencers that incorporate *hard disk recording* for acoustic parts, but that's a subject for another article; see 87). In order to synchronize acoustic parts recorded on a multitrack tape deck with the "virtual" tracks on a sequencer, a process called *tape synchronization* is used.

In this process, a *sync signal* typically is recorded on the last track of the multitrack tape (e.g., track 4, 8, or 16). One type of sync signal is called *FSK* (Frequency Shift Keying). This signal consists of two alternating frequencies recorded onto the tape from the sequencer. The rate at which they alternate correlates to the tempo of the sequence.

As shown in **Fig. 2.3**, this usually is accomplished with a device called a *sync converter*, which takes the MIDI Clocks from the sequencer and converts them into an FSK signal. This signal is recorded (or *striped*) onto the tape by playing the entire song in the sequencer, which means that the length of the composition must be decided upon and at least some of the parts must be sequenced before the sync signal is recorded. The recorded FSK signal is then played back and converted into MIDI Clocks for the sequencer, which is placed in External sync mode like the drum machine in the previous procedure. Some computer MIDI interfaces provide a direct FSK input and output, eliminating the need for a separate sync converter.

The advantage of FSK is that it's inexpensive. The drawback is that there is no way to start the tape in the middle of a song and have the sequencer "chase" to that location. With regular FSK, the sequencer simply starts at the beginning, no matter where you are on tape. An enhanced FSK signal called *Smart FSK* includes positional information that allows the use of Song Position Pointer for this purpose. Again, some computer MIDI interfaces provide a direct Smart FSK input and output, eliminating the need for a separate unit.

PROCEDURE: TAPE SYNCHRONIZATION

1. Make the appropriate audio and MIDI connections between the sequencer, sync converter, and tape recorder, as shown in **Fig. 2.3**. In particular, connect the MIDI Out of the sequencer to the MIDI In of the sync box.

2. Place the sequencer in Master or Internal sync mode.

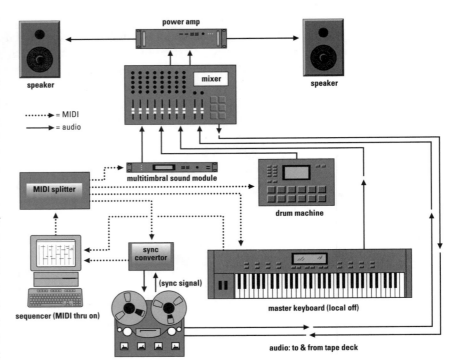

3. On the tape deck, enable the Record function on the sync track.

4. Press Play on the sequencer.

5. On the tape deck, adjust the input level for the sync track to read between 0 and +3.

6. Press Stop on the sequencer and then Rewind.

7. On the tape deck, press Record.

8. On the sequencer, press Play.

9. When the song is finished, wait a few extra seconds and press Stop on the tape deck.

10. Press Rewind on the sequencer and the tape deck.

11. Disconnect the sequencer's MIDI Out from the sync converter's MIDI In and connect the keyboard's MIDI Out to the sync converter's MIDI In. This allows you to sequence additional parts while the sequencer is synched to tape.

12. Place the sequencer in External or MIDI sync mode and press Play or Record.

13. On the tape deck, disable the Record function on the sync track and press Play. The sequencer will start playing.

14. You now can record any acoustic parts on the other tape tracks while the sequenced parts play. You also can record new parts into the sequencer.

Figure 2.3 A sequencing and tape-sync system. The sync converter accepts MIDI Clocks from the sequencer and sends a sync signal to be recorded on the tape deck. The sync signal is then converted back into MIDI Clocks and sent to the sequencer, which synchronizes to the tape as it plays. You must switch the connection on the sync converter's MIDI In from the sequencer's MIDI Out to the keyboard's MIDI Out in order to sequence additional parts while synched to tape.

Most professionals use *SMPTE time code* rather than FSK. Developed by the Society of Motion Picture and Television Engineers, this sync signal represents the passage of time in hours, minutes, seconds, and frames. It allows sequencers to start playing at any point in the song based on the tape's position. Although this format reflects its intended use with film and video, more music-only studios are using SMPTE time code because of its reliability and standardization throughout the industry.

Typically, a sync converter is required to use SMPTE with sequencers. However, the procedure is slightly different. It often is more convenient to stripe SMPTE time code for the entire length of the tape and specify different SMPTE time values for each song. This can be done before any parts are sequenced because the time code represents absolute time rather than relative time. Otherwise, the procedure for using SMPTE is much the same as it is for FSK. Once again, some of the most sophisticated computer MIDI interfaces provide a direct SMPTE input and output and require no external devices.

STOP

Now that you have a basic understanding of the fundamentals of sequencing, try it for yourself. There's no substitute for the teacher of experience. And remember: The tools of electronic music exist to help us develop our ideas, not to intimidate us into creative stagnation. So go ahead, show them who's the boss around your studio! ♪

Tips From the Pros: The Virtuoso Sequencist

BY DAN PHILLIPS

The study of the sequencer is currently so general, and good sequencists so numerous, that mediocrity on this instrument is no longer endured. In this volume will be found the exercises necessary for the acquirement of agility, independence, strength, and perfect quantization, as well as suppleness of the controllers—all indispensable qualities for fine execution. When these exercises have been mastered, difficulties will disappear as if by enchantment, and that beautiful, clear, clean, pearling execution will have been acquired which is the secret of distinguished artists."—*from the introduction to C.L. Hanon's* The Virtuoso Pianist *(slightly revised)*.

Unlike Hanon's classic book of piano exercises, we can't promise that reading this article will promote absolute mastery of your instrument. (These days, truth-in-advertising laws are very strict.) However, we *can* reveal sequencing secrets from some distinguished artists that will inspire you to greater creative heights. Fair enough?

THE PERFECTION OBSESSION

One of the reasons sequencers are so attractive is that they provide the user with the means to correct every nuance of a performance. Given the necessary patience and time, a take that previously would have been just good enough can be tweaked to perfection. However, not everyone agrees that perfection is necessarily a good thing.

"I think that when you indulge in a lot of attention to detail, it's easy to get protective of your work, and you can't see the woods for the trees," says Thomas Dolby, a certified icon of intellectual synth-pop. "Someone else could come in and make one big swipe and really improve your work. But since you're so wedded to those details, you couldn't see other possibilities."

To avoid this syndrome, Dolby creates several alternative versions of the same song. "Using *Vision*'s ability to assign a sequence to each letter on the Macintosh keyboard, I end up with different letters of the alphabet representing different approaches to the song," he says. "Then, at the push of a button, I can make comparisons. For example, with 'Pulp Culture' [a song on Dolby's album *Aliens Ate My Buick*], I did half a dozen different mixes, with slightly different grooves and drum patterns and things. I had my Mac in my dining room, and I would just wander around and make some phone calls, hit button E, watch some TV, try Q, and so on. Over a period of time, my instincts told me that F was the best version."

44

Making Music With Your Computer

Keeping an open mind about "happy accidents" is another way to avoid the perfection obsession. Rough arrangements may have more power than polished versions, and scratch tracks may end up being better than painstakingly recorded final takes.

"I finished the lyrics for 'Cruel' [from his album *Astronauts & Heretics*] very late one night," explains Dolby. "I had just bought *Studio Vision,* so I decided to sing a rough vocal right there. However, I was a bit worried about the neighbors, so I sang very softly. To save space on the hard disk, I later stripped silence [a process that removes all dead space between audio events]. If you're careless with levels, the softer sounds get clipped. Months later, I spent about four days doing the real vocal in the studio and decided to see if the rough vocal had any parts that were superior. Well, the entire rough take was better than the track I'd spent four days slaving over. Purists might raise their eyebrows when they hear it, because the sound is very clipped [by the silence stripping], as if it has a heavy noise gate on it. But that added to the distinctive vibe of the whole thing."

ON/OFF THE BEAT

Quantization and other forms of rhythmic correction tend to comprise a large part of the fine-tuning process. Unfortunately, what you see on your sequencer screen and what comes out of your speakers may not always correspond exactly.

For example, an instrument's MIDI response time—the time it takes to actually start a note after receiving a Note On message—is never zero. In fact, it can be more than 10 milliseconds per note. For the most part, you can compensate for this delay by shifting a track slightly ahead of the beat within the sequencer. However, the delay is not always constant (it varies according to the number of oscillators used and the number of notes played), which makes total correction difficult.

Erasure's Vince Clarke believes that MIDI response time is a major problem, and thus made an interesting decision for the band's latest album, *Chorus:* He abandoned MIDI. "I felt, and people also told me, that the albums I made maybe eight years ago had a very different feel from the albums I've done more recently. I think

Thomas Dolby

one of the reasons for this change was the use of MIDI."

Clarke also points out that MIDI is a *serial* protocol, which means that all MIDI events occur one after another even if they are meant to be simultaneous. This usually poses no problem at all; a single Note On event consists of three bytes transmitted at a rate of 31,250 bits per second. This means that each Note On event takes just under one millisecond to transmit. If three notes are intended to sound simultaneously, it takes nearly three milliseconds to transmit them. But because we perceive separate events as simultaneous if they are less than 10 to 20 milliseconds apart, these three notes sound like the coincident chord they are supposed to be.

However, if 32 notes are intended to sound simultaneously, there is a perceptible delay between the first and last notes, producing a slight "flam" effect rather than 32 simultaneous notes. According to Clarke, "Basically, this means that no one has made an album that's actually in perfect time in the last five years. I thought it would be nice to do one, you know?"

Although there are those who would argue that this effect is insignificant, Clarke remains convinced of its importance. To achieve the effect he wanted, he recorded the entire album with a Roland MC-4, a digitally controlled analog sequencer. Although the arrangements and pre-sequences were recorded into a MIDI sequencer, all MIDI information was converted to analog signals through several

Roland MPU-101s (MIDI-to-CV/gate converters). The control voltages and gates were then fed into the MC-4, which played the analog synths that were then recorded to tape. Experts may question this approach, but Clarke is convinced. "I don't think I'll ever use MIDI again [in the studio]," states Clarke.

Of course, not all musical styles or tastes demand that every note be perfectly quantized. Rough and ready grooves that wander off the beat can form the basis of a different aesthetic.

"I'm not interested in making perfect, homogeneous groove records. I want the human element in there, even if it's created by a malfunctioning computer," submits Trent Reznor, the driving force behind the industrial dance sound of Nine Inch Nails. "Sometimes a sequence is imperfectly quantized, so it's out of sync. Although you didn't shoot for that, you may realize that the mistakes make the track stand out. I was always pro-drum machine because they were no hassle, no screwups, perfect. But after working with real drummers, I saw there was something cool about finding that groove and how subtle off-time things can really affect the way you listen to the music. Subconsciously, you start to pick up on how things fit together. So now I simulate some of that electronically and just work with things that aren't perfect."

PUSH ME/PULL YOU

Some tools offer more than perfection, inviting real-time interaction. One of the earliest ways to invoke the excitement of indeterminacy was with arpeggiators. Rock-fusion pioneer and TV soundtrack king Jan Hammer is still finding new possibilities there.

"I've been doing all kinds of things with the Oberheim Cyclone [a flexible, programmable arpeggiator module]," he says. "You throw something at it and it throws something back at you. It's a very interesting, interactive thing. I like to just play and instinctively respond to the computer responding to me, and so on. I've been using it to work up all kinds of semi-classical parts. I'll have the texture of a string orchestra, and then do solo violin fills and runs that are being pulsed by the Cyclone in all kinds of interesting polyrhythms. It's

Erasure (Vince Clarke on right)

a lot of experimentation and trial and error, but when that sort of thing clicks, it's just magic."

Hammer, who is also a *Studio Vision* user, points out a unique potential of the hard disk recording/sequencer medium: the ability to use and copy only the best sections of a recording take. "I am a submediocre guitar player, but I can play eight measures of a rhythm part that sounds fairly decent. When I start playing, I'll definitely sound very rough at the beginning, until I get into some sort of a rhythm. So I can record into *Studio Vision* and play along until I find the groove. Then I can throw out the part where I was warming up and go straight into the good part, which is something that would be nearly impossible with tape."

This trick also can be accomplished with purely MIDI sequenced tracks. If you find that you keep warming up to a difficult part just as it's almost over, make the section longer, copy the good part to the beginning, and then cut the extra measures out.

BRAVE NEW RHYTHMS

Industrial, rap, hip-hop, house, and other new music styles often rely heavily on rhythm tracks sampled from other recordings. While this occasionally produces synergistic collages, it more often degenerates into clichéd quotes. However, sampling doesn't have to be a passive process. A sample can be transformed into something new and personal by processing it with effects or software-synthesis programs such as Digidesign's *Turbosynth*.

"I'll find, say, a drum loop and try to turn it into something interesting that sounds nothing like the original," says Reznor. "I'll *Turbosynth* it, distort it through the board, tune it up or down, or even EQ everything out except one frequency. On 'Get Down Make Love' [the B-side of the *Sin* 12-inch release], all of the loops are the same sample run through different *Turbosynth* patches and started at different points in the measure. This produced the cool, clanky, chunky kind of a beat that drives the track."

Of course, sequenced rhythms don't have to come from samples or even from drums. Session synthesist Larry Fast likes to create rhythms from timbral shifts on a synth patch. "I'll use a psuedo-analog sound on the Yamaha SY77 and set up a patch that allows me to control the filter using MIDI continuous controllers in real time," he says. "Then I record different continuous controller values into the sequencer and create a rhythm by using the sequenced controller messages to modulate the filter with a sample-and-hold effect [abruptly moving from one level to another]. Basically, I'm emulating what I used to do with a Moog modular system. I also use rhythmic Wave Sequences on the Korg Wavestation."

Even if a synth doesn't allow you to route a MIDI modulator to the filter, you still can create timbral rhythms. For instance, you can design a patch in which velocity controls the filter cutoff but has little or no effect on amplitude. You then can use this patch to record a rhythmic part, varying your velocity accents widely for a simulated sample-and-hold effect.

If your synth responds to MIDI System Exclusive in real time, and your sequencer can record, edit, and play back SysEx messages in the middle of a track, you can use these messages in place of *bona fide* continuous controllers. It takes a bit of hacking around in hexadecimal numbers, but the results are worth the trouble.

My Roland JX-8P can send out SysEx messages whenever a parameter is edited. I simply call up the filter-cutoff parameter for editing, put my sequencer in record, and move the synth's data-entry slider to

Jan Hammer

generate a brief stream of SysEx. I then pull out a few of these events, arrange them into a rhythmic pattern (perhaps every sixteenth note) and if necessary edit the cutoff value for each beat until the timbres create the desired pulse.

LA LIMITE

Musical instruments always have presented musicians and composers with limitations of one sort or another. After all, an instrument can play only so many notes at a time, and fingers can stretch only so far. However, our attempts to circumvent (or work within) these limitations can get the creative juices flowing and inspire us to develop unique solutions. In fact, it can be useful to create self-imposed limitations for the structure they provide. For example, Schoenberg's restrictive 12-tone system was intended to impose order on the staggering possibilities of atonality.

Clarke took a big step in this direction on Erasure's new album. All of the instrumental tracks—including drums—were created solely with analog synthesizers. Not only that, all of the tracks were monophonic. "Not using chords required more thinking about the orchestration of each piece," he notes. "The absence of chordal washes made it easier to construct more interesting sounds, rather than going completely over the top to make something that would stand out over everything. Also, these arrangements allowed the vocals a bit more room."

However, you often don't have the luxury of choosing limitations. Usually, a problem presents itself and you're forced to find a way around it. One common problem is the "not enough instruments" syndrome. Typically, I'll want one more timbre playing back, but all my available channels are already zinging away. One way to get around this problem is to create a keyboard split on one or more of the sound modules, so that more than one timbre is available on a single MIDI channel. If the instrument provides enough leeway in transposition, there's no reason that the lower part of a split must be in the bass range; you could just as easily have a lead sound on the bottom and a pad on the top.

Even with synths that are ostensibly monotimbral, you can create patches that sound very different at high and low velocities by modulating filter cutoff (or modulator amplitude in FM synths), attack time, and so on. With careful editing of velocity in the sequencer, you can use the same patch to simultaneously produce a pad and a percussive bass line, or mellow chords and a bright lead line.

NEW CONTROLLERS

While MIDI was originally designed to represent human performance gestures on a keyboard controller, it also can be used to create gestures that are outside the capabilities of either the human player or the controller itself. "I used the new Roland RSS system [a 3-D spatial sound processor, see **Fig. 2.4**] on my *Hotel Luna* album and achieved infinitely more drama by using MIDI control rather than the unit's manual rotary knobs," explains Private Music artist Suzanne Ciani. She simply sent discontinuous MIDI Control Change values to the RSS. "MIDI control allowed the spatial effects to jump all over the place in ways that would be impossible to get by simply turning knobs."

In fact, the concept of a "controller" is getting increasingly fuzzy. Sure, we still have keyboards, but we also have software such as *sYbil* and Opcode's *Max*, which transform simple human gestures into complex, multi-event MIDI datastreams

that can be captured in a sequencer and edited. Jan Hammer also points out that there are controllers lurking where we might not think to look.

"I'll use anything for a controller," Hammer laughs. "Sometimes I'll use the little keyboard that's onscreen in Opcode's *Galaxy* to play something and record it as a MIDI file. There are all kinds of things on that keyboard—you can control the repeat rate, or just gliss the cursor across the keys, which you would not be able to play. You can use 'impossible' performance gestures like that, record them into a sequencer, and take them even further. You also can map drum pads with interesting note assignments and just start bashing drum patterns. You'd be amazed at what comes out. You don't need a conventional controller to make interesting music."

THE FINAL PASS

As with any form of musical production, the glory of sequencing is in the results. Whatever triggers the creative process is a good thing; how it's accomplished is not the issue. Learn to experiment and seek out unique solutions to technical limitations. And remember that a controller doesn't necessarily have to be a *standard* controller (it is possible that the weirder the instrument, the better the results). Practice with your sequencer, get to know its quirks, and you eventually may acquire the "pearling execution" of the Virtuoso Sequencist. ♪

Figure 2.4 Roland's RSS system

What is General MIDI?

When MIDI came into being, no one had any idea that it eventually would dominate the music-making process. The goal of Sequential Circuits' 1981 proposal for the Universal Synthesizer Interface was sound layering and control from a single remote keyboard or sequencer. Crossbreeding with Roland's Digital Control Bus raised the ante to sixteen instruments, with room for growth in control capabilities. At the time, manufacturers were still groping for applications and customers.

Today, MIDI is branching out, poking its head into such areas as mix automation, lighting control, and even tape transports. MIDI also has the opportunity to revolutionize the way consumers experience music.

At a meeting of the MIDI Manufacturers Association (MMA) few years ago, Warner New Media, a division of Warner Communications, introduced the idea of a standardized subset of the MIDI protocols. *General MIDI* would let a consumer run a MIDI cable from a sequence player to a sound module and have a predictable set of sounds come out the other end.

The original target was CD+M, or CD+MIDI, a variation of CD audio that encodes MIDI data in parallel with sound. The group also had an eye on CD-Interactive, a new entertainment system which began shipping in the fall of 1992.

BY CHRIS MEYER

At the time, most MMA members, including myself, met the proposal with disinterest. We felt MIDI was only for musicians and didn't want such "restrictions" placed on our instruments.

Fortunately, the interested parties persisted. Passport Designs and a growing army of companies finally convinced the association to adopt the proposal. General MIDI Level 1 also was ratified recently by the JMSC (Japanese MIDI Standards Committee). The General MIDI standard is useful for making a predictable entity of a MIDI sound module. But like MIDI itself, the possible applications for General MIDI (GM) have expanded far beyond this initial purpose.

THE PROBLEM

Synthesizers are designed to make a variety of unique sounds. MIDI, on the other hand, was created so that two connected instruments would perform exactly the same way.

This basic difference plagues every person who uses MIDI with instruments from different manufacturers. You have to translate the capabilities and presets from one synth to another. In the simplest case, you just learn which program numbers bring up a particular sound on each instrument. (Let's see: The strings are MIDI program number 8 on Synth A, which it displays as 21 on the front panel, and program number 37 on Synth B, which it displays as 38. No problem.) More advanced cases may include matching pitch bend ratios and other esoterica. Most of us have figured out how to do this, but we've had to become MIDI engineers in the process.

Standard MIDI Files (see "Standard MIDI Files," p. 55) have made this translation problem more obvious. SMFs made the promise that we could exchange sequences and collaborate in new ways. But we found that the process required us to become experts on our collaborators' rigs as well as our own. (What's that funky marimba line? I thought Larry said the horns took the lead!)

THE SOLUTION

The heart of GM is the *Instrument Patch Map*, shown in **Table 1**. This is a list of 128 sounds with corresponding MIDI program numbers. Most of these are imitative sounds, though the list includes synth sounds, ethnic instruments, and a handful of sound effects.

The sounds fall roughly into sixteen families of eight variations each. Grouping sounds like this makes it easy to reorchestrate a piece using similar sounds. The Instrument Map isn't the final word on musical instruments of the world, but it's pretty complete.

General MIDI also includes a *Percussion Key Map*, shown in **Table 2**. This mapping derives from the Roland/Sequential mapping used on early drum machines. As with the Instrument Map, it doesn't cover every percussive instrument in the world, but it's more than adequate as a basic set.

To avoid concerns with channels, General MIDI restricts percussion to MIDI Channel 10. Theoretically, only the lower nine channels are for the instruments, but the GM spec states that a sound module must respond to all sixteen MIDI channels, with dynamic voice allocation and a minimum of 24 voices of polyphony.

The GM standard doesn't mention sound quality or synthesis methods. Discussions are underway on standardizing sound parameters such as playable range and envelope times. This will ensure that an arrangement that relies on phrasing and balance can play back on a variety of modules.

Other requirements for a GM sound module include response to velocity, modulation wheel, aftertouch, sustain pedal, expression pedal, main volume and pan, and the All Notes Off and Reset All Controllers messages. The module also must respond to both Pitch Bend and Pitch Bend Sensitivity (a MIDI registered parameter). The default Pitch Bend range is ±2 semitones.

Middle C (C3) corresponds to MIDI key 60, and master tuning must be adjustable. Finally, the MMA created a new Universal System Exclusive message to turn General MIDI on and off (for devices that might have "consumer" and "programmable" settings). **Table 3** summarizes these requirements.

General MIDI also has room for future expansion, including additional drum and instrument assignments and more required controllers.

APPLICATIONS

Multimedia is all about blurring the lines between different forms of art and entertainment, and General MIDI is a perfect multimedia standard for music. General MIDI gives musicians a chance to share our talents in new areas.

• **Home Entertainment** The purpose of CD+MIDI is to put MIDI-encoded recreations of instrumental parts, or bonus instrumental lines, on an otherwise normal audio CD. Users can try their hand at reorchestration, or explore alternate versions. MIDI is also listed as a future extension for CD-Interactive.

Now that General MIDI finally exists, this medium is ready to take off. Roland's Sound Canvas is the first GM sound module, with more to follow. Standard MIDI File players, such as Roland's Sound Brush, are also available.

Musicians who create most of their music with MIDI should be particularly interested in exploiting CD+MIDI and General MIDI to create "deeper" records that listeners can experience with a greater degree of participation.

• **Games** Many computer games rely on synthesizer chips or MIDI sound modules to create sound effects and music. Most popular are Yamaha FM sound chips (such as the Sound Blaster card for the IBM PC) and variations of the Roland MT-32 (including the CM-32 module and LAPC-1 IBM PC card). However, these two families of targets are incompatible. In addition, until recently there were no standards for sampled sound playback on PCs. Most game companies created their instruments and sound effects by using MIDI System Exclusive codes to reprogram the sound modules. As sound chips evolve, game companies must continually reprogram to support different modules and cards.

Enter the Microsoft MPC (Multimedia PC) standard (see "Multimedia Windows for the PC," p. 113). While retaining compatibility with existing cards, it presents a set of sound specs that include support of General MIDI and standardized sample rates and formats. (*Multimedia Windows* also can play Standard MIDI Files in the background.) This means that game companies can use General MIDI for normal music and background orchestration and store custom samples for sound effects and voices in a standard format.

• **Music Publishing and Distribution** Music can take the form of finished recordings or sets of marks and codes on paper for humans to play. There aren't many options for people who want to explore music but have neither the time nor skill to endure several years of learning to play an instrument.

Electronic-music pioneer Morton Subotnick has been working on this problem at the Center for Experiments in Art, Information, and Technology at Cal Arts. He has demonstrated a system consisting of a computer and synthesizer with which a person can interact with a piece of music in one of several ways: conducting tempo and phrasing while the computer plays the actual notes, playing one of the parts while following the computer, playing one of the parts and have the computer follow him or her, or playing the entire piece him- or herself.

Not only is this great for practicing musicians, but it gives non-musicians a way to exercise control over music as well.

CD players that can output MIDI (the NEC/Passport MIDIWorld player and Commodore's CDTV) are already in production. It is inevitable that General MIDI will be the playback standard for MIDI CDs. As a result, interactive music lessons and new forms of music publishing are becoming realistic possibilities.

• **Professional Collaboration** Have you ever tried to exchange Standard MIDI Files with someone using different equipment? How about recalling a song you worked on months ago and trying to remember what sounds were loaded in which synths? With the GM Instrument and

ROLAND'S GS STANDARD

When Warner New Media first proposed a General MIDI Standard, most MMA members gave it little thought. But as discussions proceeded, Roland listened and developed a sound module to meet the new specification. At the same NAMM show where the MMA ratified General MIDI Level 1, Roland showed Sound Brush and Sound Canvas, a Standard MIDI File player and a GM-compatible sound module.

To satisfy companies who felt that General MIDI didn't go far enough, Roland created a superset of General MIDI Level 1 called GS Standard. It obeys all the protocols and sound maps of General MIDI and adds many extra controllers and sounds. Some of the controllers use Unregistered Parameter Numbers to give macro control over synth parameters such as envelope attack and decay rates.

The new MIDI Bank Select message provides access to extra sounds (including variations on the stock sounds and a re-creation of the MT-32 factory patches). The programs in each bank align with the original 128 in General MIDI's Instrument Patch Map, with eight banks housing related families. The GS Standard also includes a "fallback" system. If the Sound Canvas receives a request for a bank/program number combination that does not exist, it will reassign it to the master instrument in that family. A set of Roland System Exclusive messages allows reconfiguration and customization of the sound module.

This means that a Roland GS Standard sound module will correctly play back any song designed for General MIDI. In addition, if the song's creator wants to incorporate some extra nuances, they can include the GS Standard extensions in the sequence. None of these extensions are so radical as to make the song unplayable on a normal GM sound module, however. After all, compatibility is what MIDI—and especially General MIDI—is all about.

1-8	Piano	33-40	Bass	65-72	Reed	97-104	Synth Effects
1	Acoustic Grand Piano	33	Acoustic Bass	65	Soprano Sax	97	FX 1 (rain)
2	Bright Acoustic Piano	34	Electric Bass (finger)	66	Alto Sax	98	FX 2 (soundtrack)
3	Electric Grand Piano	35	Electric Bass (pick)	67	Tenor Sax	99	FX 3 (crystal)
4	Honky-tonk Piano	36	Fretless Bass	68	Baritone Sax	100	FX 4 (atmosphere)
5	Electric Piano 1	37	Slap Bass 1	69	Oboe	101	FX 5 (brightness)
6	Electric Piano 2	38	Slap Bass 2	70	English Horn	102	FX 6 (goblins)
7	Harpsichord	39	Synth Bass 1	71	Bassoon	103	FX 7 (echoes)
8	Clav	40	Synth Bass 2	72	Clarinet	104	FX 8 (sci-fi)
9-16	Chrom Percussion	41-48	Strings	73-80	Pipe	105-112	Ethnic
9	Celesta	41	Violin	73	Piccolo	105	Sitar
10	Glockenspiel	42	Viola	74	Flute	106	Banjo
11	Music Box	43	Cello	75	Recorder	107	Shamisen
12	Vibraphone	44	Contrabass	76	Pan Flute	108	Koto
13	Marimba	45	Tremolo Strings	77	Blown Bottle	109	Kalimba
14	Xylophone	46	Pizzicato Strings	78	Shakuhachi	110	Bagpipe
15	Tubular Bells	47	Orchestral Strings	79	Whistle	111	Fiddle
16	Dulcimer	48	Timpani	80	Ocarina	112	Shanai
17-24	Organ	49-56	Ensemble	81-88	Synth Lead	113-120	Percussive
17	Drawbar Organ	49	String Ensemble 1	81	Lead 1 (square)	113	Tinkle Bell
18	Percussive Organ	50	String Ensemble 2	82	Lead 2 (sawtooth)	114	Agogo
19	Rock Organ	51	SynthStrings 1	83	Lead 3 (calliope)	115	Steel Drums
20	Church Organ	52	SynthStrings 2	84	Lead 4 (chiff)	116	Woodblock
21	Reed Organ	53	Choir Aahs	85	Lead 5 (charang)	117	Taiko Drum
22	Accordion	54	Voice Oohs	86	Lead 6 (voice)	118	Melodic Tom
23	Harmonica	55	Synth Voice	87	Lead 7 (fifths)	119	Synth Drum
24	Tango Accordion	56	Orchestra Hit	88	Lead 8 (bass+lead)	120	Reverse Cymbal
25-32	Guitar	57-64	Brass	89-96	Synth Pad	121-128	Sound Effects
25	Acoustic Guitar (nylon)	57	Trumpet	89	Pad 1 (new age)	121	Guitar Fret Noise
26	Acoustic Guitar (steel)	58	Trombone	90	Pad 2 (warm)	122	Breath Noise
27	Electric Guitar (jazz)	59	Tuba	91	Pad 3 (polysynth)	123	Seashore
28	Electric Guitar (clean)	60	Muted Trumpet	92	Pad 4 (choir)	124	Bird Tweet
29	Electric Guitar (muted)	61	French Horn	93	Pad 5 (bowed)	125	Telephone Ring
30	Overdriven Guitar	62	Brass Section	94	Pad 6 (metallic)	126	Helicopter
31	Distortion Guitar	63	SynthBrass 1	95	Pad 7 (halo)	127	Applause
32	Guitar Harmonics	64	SynthBrass 2	96	Pad 8 (sweep)	128	Gunshot

Table 1 The General MIDI Instrument Map groups sounds into sixteen families, with eight instruments in each family.

Key	Drum Sound	Key	Drum Sound	Key	Drum Sound
35	Acoustic Bass Drum	51	Ride Cymbal 1	67	High Agogo
36	Bass Drum 1	52	Chinese Cymbal	68	Low Agogo
37	Side Stick	53	Ride Bell	69	Cabasa
38	Acoustic Snare	54	Tambourine	70	Maracas
39	Hand Clap	55	Splash Cymbal	71	Short Whistle
40	Electric Snare	56	Cowbell	72	Long Whistle
41	Low Floor Tom	57	Crash Cymbal 2	73	Short Guiro
42	Closed Hi-Hat	58	Vibraslap	74	Long Guiro
43	High Floor Tom	59	Ride Cymbal 2	75	Claves
44	Pedal Hi-Hat	60	Hi Bongo	76	Hi Wood Block
45	Low Tom	61	Low Bongo	77	Low Wood Block
46	Open Hi-Hat	62	Mute Hi Conga	78	Mute Cuica
47	Low-Mid Tom	63	Open Hi Conga	79	Open Cuica
48	Hi-Mid Tom	64	Low Conga	80	Mute Triangle
49	Crash Cymbal 1	65	High Timbale	81	Open Triangle
50	High Tom	66	Low Timbale		

Percussion Key Maps, electronic musicians possess a usable template for exchanging or recalling sequences and hearing them more or less as they were intended to be played.

Think of General MIDI as the missing link for interchanging Standard MIDI Files. Today's computer modems allow you to call someone up and jam, and a standardized mapping of sounds makes this hookup and translation much easier. And you always can go back and assign custom sounds for the final mix.

It behooves all of us to look into a GM setup for our own studios, so we finally can work with each other at the drop of a 5-pin DIN cable and 3.5-inch diskette. Also expect to see a burgeoning market in third-party sounds that re-create the GM Instrument Map on a variety of existing instruments.

THE FUTURE

General MIDI could prove to be as revolutionary as MIDI itself. Any industry needs standards, and General MIDI completes the standard description of a piece of music. Its existence means that anything that uses music can have a common language with which to interact, at least before the final recording.

General MIDI does not mean that every MIDI instrument must follow the GM Instrument and Percussion Key Maps. Synths will still be synths, and are expected to be different from each other. General MIDI is just a set of rules that ensures that "consumer" modules will react as expected. And of course, you don't *have* to use General MIDI; many may find such a basic standard too confining. Remember, however, that GM is not just for people who can't set the time on their VCRs.

For more information on General MIDI, you can obtain a copy of the Level 1 Specification document ($5) from the International MIDI Association, 5316 West 57th St., Los Angeles, CA 90056; tel. (310) 649-6434. You also might want to order the first issue of the Journal of the MMA (back issues: $15), which contains an article from Passport Designs and MIDI activist Stanley Jungleib on General MIDI. If you feel particularly motivated, join the MMA (same address as IMA) and participate in further evolving any or all facets of MIDI. ♪

Table 2 The GM Percussion Key Map assigns drum sounds to individual note numbers. MIDI Channel 10 is reserved for percussion.

Voices A minimum of either 24 fully dynamically allocated voices are available simultaneously for both melodic and percussive sounds or sixteen dynamically allocated voices for melody plus eight more voices for percussion.

Channels General MIDI mode supports all sixteen MIDI channels. Each channel can play a variable number of voices (polyphony). Each channel can play a different instrument (timbre). Key-based percussion is always on channel 10.

Instruments A minimum of sixteen different timbres play various instrument sounds. There are a minimum of 128 presets for Instruments (MIDI program numbers).

Note on/Note off
Octave registration: middle C = MIDI Key 60. All voices including percussion respond to velocity.

Controllers

Controller #	Description
1	Modulation
7	Main Volume
10	Pan
11	Expression
64	Sustain
121	Reset All Controllers
123	All Notes Off

Registered Parameters

Parameter #	Description
0	Pitch Bend Sensitivity
1	Fine Tuning
2	Coarse Tuning

Additional Channel Messages

Channel Pressure (Aftertouch)	Pitch Bend

Power-Up Defaults

Pitch Bend amount = 0	Volume = 90
Pitch Bend Sensitivity = ± 2 semitones	All other Controllers are reset

Table 3 The minimum requirements of a General MIDI-compatible instrument.

Standard MIDI Files

Virtually all sequencer manufacturers and developers now support Standard MIDI Files, and with good reason. They provide the easiest way to transfer sequences between different programs (including notation programs) and different computers. Standard MIDI Files (SMFs) also have encouraged the development of algorithmic composition, drum-pattern programming, and other types of esoteric software. SMFs make it a snap for these programs to export the music they create into general-purpose applications. This article will take a look at the SMF format and how it's being implemented by sequencer and notation programs. As you'll see, this implementation varies widely.

SMF CITY

SMFs include two types of data: MIDI and non-MIDI. Not surprisingly, MIDI performance data and any related SysEx messages make up the majority of most files. (Not all SMF-compatible sequencers can read SysEx within an SMF, however.) SMFs also can include special non-MIDI information, called meta-events (see sidebar, "Meet the Meta-Events"). Meta-events include things such as track names and tempo and time-signature changes. As with SysEx, support for these meta-events

is not universal, but this doesn't mean you won't be able to hear your music after transferring it to another machine or program. It simply will confuse matters.

Here's a common problem: You transfer an SMF from one sequencer to another, and you lose your track names and tempo changes. Which sequencer is to blame? Your first test should be to create an SMF in the source sequencer and import it back into the same sequencer. Any information lost during this out-and-right-back-in transfer probably was not put into the SMF by your sequencer in the first place, so there's no point in blaming the second sequencer for "ignoring" nothing. This test also will show you if different tracks assigned to the same channel are merged in your sequencer, and what happens to looped tracks in the SMF.

If this test leaves the track names and tempo changes intact, shift your focus to the second sequencer. Two options are possible: Either the second sequencer doesn't support these messages, or the information is being encoded into a different type of meta-event than the sequencer expects. For instance, track names have their own meta-event, but some programs use the text meta-event instead. If the source sequencer stores them as text and the destination looks for them as track-

BY
DAVID (RUDY)
TRUBITT

name events, they'll be lost in the translation. Some programs offer the thoughtful option of selecting text or track-name events for onscreen track names so you can work around the limitations of other programs.

Very few programs support all, or even most, of the currently defined meta-events. (One exception is provided by Opcode, who were instrumental in the adoption of the SMF format. *Vision*'s meta-event support is very complete.) Although support for all events is not a requirement for a "proper" implementation of SMFs, the more the better.

That said, there are some parts of the SMF 1.0 spec that have never caught on. For example, most programs support both format 0 and format 1 files, which represent single-track and multitrack sequences respectively. However, almost no one supports format 2 SMFs, which are akin to a collection of format 0 sequences in a single file. Within SMFs, the time between events can be expressed as fractions of a quarter note or in a time code-based representation. But support for time code-based SMFs is almost nonexistent.

There are orphans among the meta-events as well. Support for cue points, SMPTE offsets, and lyrics are rare.

SHUTTLE DIPLOMACY
Lost meta-event information can be replaced manually once you've loaded a sequence, but if you're sending the same SMF back and forth repeatedly, you'll have to make the fix each time. Unfortunately, not much can be done to avoid this, but knowing which events will and won't survive the transfer can help you choose the way you annotate your sequences.

Here are a few problems you may come across. Consider a sequencer that reads cue or marker events but transforms them into text events. If you write that sequence as an SMF, the resulting file won't have any marker events in it—they'll be mixed in with other text events in the sequence. Data also can vanish when the program preserves only the first or last instance of a particular meta-event. For example, *Texture* recognizes tempo change events, but

only the first one in a file. Similarly, *Cadenza* preserves only the last text event it receives on a given track, discarding all earlier ones, and *Cakewalk* recognizes only the first key-signature event.

In order to read tempo change and time signature information correctly, some programs require these "conductor" events to appear in the first track (in fact, the SMF spec recommends this). A related situation occurs with Dr. T's *KCS* and *Tiger Cub* sequencers. These programs assume that the conductor track is as long as the longest track in the sequence. If the incoming SMF has only one tempo event at the beginning of the sequence, the programs will appear to get stuck on the first note because they think that event represents the end of the sequence. You can work around this problem by lengthening the conductor track after loading the SMF.

Different internal resolutions also can result in round-off errors between sequencers. For instance, 192 ppqn does not divide evenly into 480 ppqn, and moving sequences between these resolutions can cause notes to be shifted slightly.

COMPUTER TRANSLATIONS
As you've seen, moving SMFs between programs on a single computer isn't necessarily trivial. But what about moving an SMF to a different type of computer? You could always just connect the MIDI Out of one computer to the MIDI In of another and not use SMFs, but that's not the most convenient method, even if you've got the two computers in the same room. Two better approaches are serial transfer of a SMF file (through a direct cable, via a network, or via modem) or floppy-disk exchange.

If you have the appropriate transfer software, serial transfers should be straightforward. However, you must be careful to use a file transfer protocol that preserves the integrity of binary data files. Never use the protocols intended for "text" files; you'll get garbage.

Floppy-disk exchange can be very easy or more complicated, depending on the computers involved. First, the easy stuff. PCs with 3.5-inch drives and Atari STs share the same basic disk format, so SMFs on disk can be easily swapped between these machines. (STs can only read 720K disks, however.) Amiga disk formats also are somewhat similar, but the Amiga requires a special controller board, called a Bridgeboard, to read and write PC or ST disks.

The Macintosh is a different case, because its disk and file formats are incompatible with PCs. Thankfully, you can overcome this incompatibility on either the Mac side or the PC side. First, all of the newer Macs (from the SE/30 onward) are equipped with SuperDrives, which can read and write 3.5-inch DOS-format 1.4 MB or 720K disks when used with *Apple File Exchange*, Dayna Communications' *DOS Mounter*, or similar software. Owners of older Macs are stuck spending a fair amount of dough to purchase either an Apple or third-party external Mac drive that can read and write DOS disks. For PCs, Central Point Software offers the Deluxe Option Board, which enables your 3.5-inch floppy drive-equipped PC to read and write Mac disks.

Once files have been transferred successfully to a Mac floppy or hard drive, you have to deal with the Mac's file formats, regardless of whether you used modems, serial cables, or floppy disks to make the transfer. Macintosh files include information on the file type and the file creator in a special header at the beginning of the file (this, by the way, is the information used to determine which document icons are shown on the desktop). Unfortunately, an SMF from a non-Mac computer won't include this "creator" information and will show up as a plain document file on the Mac desktop. Even worse, your Mac sequencer won't even try to open such a file, because it will think (incorrectly) that it doesn't contain the right type of data.

Fixing the problem is simple once you know how. Two four-letter codes identify the file's type and creator. Just change the file's type to "Midi" (this data is case-sensitive, so enter it exactly as shown). This can be done using a number of programs, including Apple's *ResEdit* or Central Point's *Mac Tools*. Once you have corrected the problem, your sequencer will let you load

MEET THE META-EVENTS

*H*ere is a list of the meta-events defined in Version 1.0 of the SMF spec, along with a brief description of their purpose. In addition, we've listed the percentage of support for the various events, based on an informal survey of 26 software developers.

- **End of Track (100%)** This mandatory meta-event specifies the end of each track.
- **Sequence/Track Name (80%)** This event preserves the descriptive names you designate for your tracks.
- **Set Tempo (76%)** Multiple ST events in an SMF affect tempo changes, although not all programs can accept more than one. Some programs also require them to be in track 1.
- **Time Signature (73%)** Multiple TS events also are allowed, although I found occasional problems with handling time signatures other than 4/4.
- **Key Signature (58%)** This is useful to notation programs, which, incidentally, support even fewer meta-events than sequencers.
- **Text Event (50%)** The most general way to put comments into an SMF is with text events. As mentioned in the main text, some sequencers use text events for track names, but a better use of this event probably is for general comments.
- **Copyright Notice (27%)** You could put copyright notices in text events or a track name, although empty tracks with names may be lost in translation. This event probably is of most interest to those who distribute SMFs for sale.
- **Instrument Name (23%)** This meta-event was created to leave a message describing the sort of sound that should be used with a given track. To be safe, you should put that information in the track-name event instead.
- **MIDI Channel Prefix (19%)** A group of subsequent meta-events can be associated with a specific channel or track in a format 0 file with this meta-event.
- **Lyric (15%)** Several notation developers commented on the lyric event's lack of provisions for second and third verses. At such a low support rate, you'd better send the lyrics in a separate file, just in case.
- **Marker (15%)** Designed to mark beginnings of verses, etc., this meta-event has surprisingly low support. Note that some programs, such as Voyetra's *Sequencer Plus*, have markers that are not exported as marker events.
- **Cue Point (11%)** These are like markers, but for "hit points" (car crash, breaking glass, etc.) when synching to video.
- **SMPTE Offset (8%)** With the number of sequencers capable of synching to SMPTE, it's surprising how few packages support this event. Hopefully, this will change. In the meantime, put this vital piece of info in a (non-empty) track name.
- **Sequencer Specific (8%)** Intended for special use with packages that use SMFs as their only file format, this is like a SysEx for meta-events. It is also used by Hybrid Arts' *SMPTE Track* for interface port selection. (A new meta-event for this purpose is under discussion.)
- **Sequence Number (0%)** Last, and apparently least, is the lonely Sequence Number event, which no respondents supported.

the file and begin working. Changing the other code is not required.

This creator information also plays a role when you transfer SMFs from a Mac to a non-Mac computer. The 128-byte header containing this data must be deleted before most PC, ST, or Amiga programs can import the file. The deletion can occur either on the Mac before sending the file, or on the other computer, using one of many available utilities.

WHAT NEXT?

Standard MIDI Files aren't standing still. One new use has been found by Opcode, whose programs now can cut and paste SMFs to the Mac's clipboard just like any text or graphic. Using the clipboard avoids the extra steps of exporting an SMF to disk and then importing it into the next program. Because the clipboard is a common place for data exchange, other vendors hopefully will follow suit.

Another area being discussed within the software-development community is the transfer of scores between notation programs. The SMF spec is well-suited to exchanging sequences, but falls far short

when trying to move traditional notation. For example, there are no MIDI messages to describe stem direction or slur placement, and MIDI's note representation (Note On, Note Off) is fundamentally different than a score's single note events that embody duration.

At this point, things could go two ways. Additional meta-events describing more specific notation information could be added to the SMF spec, or an entirely new file format could be developed for exchanging scores. While new meta-events certainly can be added, most notation programs currently support far fewer meta-events than sequencers. However, creating a new format would not be an easy task, as each notation-software company has developed unique structures for storing scores.

General MIDI (see p. 49) will certainly increase the number of SMF sequences, and vendors hopefully will continue to expand their SMF meta-event support to make things easier for users. Despite incomplete implementations and the potential problems they cause, SMFs are a success: When software companies create a framework for cooperation, everyone benefits. ♪

The MIDI Trap

BY PAUL D. LEHRMAN

An article published recently in a respected independent film journal claimed that no decent film score ever would come from a MIDI studio. The author, an experienced film composer, argued that MIDI-produced music was "mechanized, quantified, [and] predigested" and could never replace the work of "real musicians." Furthermore, it stated that MIDI wasn't any cheaper than live recording.

As I make a decent portion of my living creating film scores in my MIDI studio, I was rather taken aback by this thesis. It suggested that everything I and my fellow MIDI-heads have worked on for the last decade or so—making synthesizers sound better, designing software that improves creativity, bringing professional tools into affordable price brackets, and designing elegant and cheap ways to link sound and pictures—has been for naught. But after a few days of reflection and some concentrated radio and TV listening, I began to agree with him. I do find most MIDI music—and not just music for films—predictable, mechanical, and boring. (He was dead wrong about it not being cheaper, but that's a different article.)

The writer blamed MIDI itself, however, and on this crucial point I disagree. MIDI doesn't kill music; musicians kill music.

MIDI has made it possible, even easy, to create "perfect" music, precisely programmed and absolutely identical every time it's performed. But MIDI-based music that sounds live, as if it were performed by human beings instead of machines, is a rare commodity. And only real-sounding music can communicate human values that listeners find worth listening to. This becomes more true as music ages: In 2015, "Classic Hits" radio will not be playing New Kids on the Block and Vanilla Ice.

MIDI has been a wonderfully democratizing influence, encouraging many musicians who otherwise could not possibly afford to produce good-sounding stuff to try their hand at making records, performing, scoring images, or simply enjoying themselves. It's fueled a tremendous technological revolution, inspired countless software and hardware designers and independent record labels, and created a new genre of magazines such as *Electronic Musician*.

But MIDI also has caused both manufacturers and consumers to become lazy. When it's so easy to make songs sound good, why even work at making music? That's the trap MIDI musicians have fallen into.

IS MIDI TO BLAME?

It's fashionable to complain that MIDI isn't good enough for "real" music. But in reality, despite the inevitable compromises that went into its adoption, MIDI is an extremely well-designed descriptive language for musical performance.

Before electronics, all music was created by physical gestures, such as singing, whistling, and beating. MIDI, with its carefully defined but wide-ranging command set, provides an excellent modeling system for physical gestures. A musical sound starts, it grows and changes, and then it stops. All of these actions are reflected in the MIDI command set.

Then what's the problem? Because MIDI tools do so much immediately and bring so much power to even the poorest (in both senses of the word) musicians, it's incredibly tempting to let the tools do all the work. There's an old joke about a guy who hears a certain machine will do half his work for him, and so he buys two. When the tools do all the work, however, the musician gives up the responsibility of creating, and what comes out will speak only to other tools, not other humans.

Rather than take advantage of the new opportunities MIDI technology creates, many musicians simply use it as a faster, cheaper means to the same old goals. In the process, their horizons get even smaller, and the genres they work in become even more restricted.

USER LAZINESS

The most commonly cited fault in MIDI composition is over-reliance on quantizing. Quantizing robs music of any rhythmic subtleties. And while it often helps compensate for a lack of technique, it also eliminates much of what we hear as phrasing. Phrasing is more than note durations and volumes; it's also small changes in timing: A note that's delayed slightly will seem to be emphasized, while notes that are played ahead of a beat tend to be de-emphasized. Quantizing completely destroys this effect.

Step-time entry is even worse, because durations as well as attacks are quantized. If you ever feel like taking a glorious phrase by Mozart and squeezing all the life out of it, enter it into a sequencer in step-time.

Another familiar bugbear is dependence on factory sounds. Synthesizers admittedly are hard to program, and the folks at the factory know a lot more about it than you do. But becoming a slave to their taste is a sure-fire way to lose any semblance of individuality in your music.

Factory sounds are designed to show off an instrument in a music store, to grab your attention and wrench your gut. While these qualities are useful, successfully composing, arranging, and producing a project also requires subtlety, expressiveness, and the ability to blend.

In addition, factory sounds get old fast, as a quick listen to the cheapo music behind most late-night TV ads will attest. A fundamental principle related to this phenomenon occurred to me a few years ago, after a particularly boring computer-music concert: Any sound, no matter how beautiful and complex, becomes boring if you repeat it often enough.

HALF A SPEC

Just as neurologists theorize that we normally use only a small part of our brains, most MIDI users only take advantage of a small part of the MIDI spec. How many of us have ventured beyond Note Ons and Offs, the occasional Sustain Pedal, and maybe a little Modulation Wheel or Pitch Bend? Knowing when a violin note starts and stops is only a small part of what that note is all about. So it should be with a MIDI note, but few MIDI composers bother to use footpedals for anything other than volume, or aftertouch for real-time timbral changes, or breath controllers or joysticks for anything. Ask yourself: Do you even know how to program your synths to respond to that kind of control?

Finding or designing the perfect sound too often becomes the only goal: We just hit a key and walk away while the music unfolds by itself. But music is not what happens when you push a button; music is what you do with the sound *after* the button is pushed. Every note that comes from a saxophone is unique; the pitch, vibrato, tone, and volume contour all differ. How dare we play a few notes on a keyboard and call it a sax line!

Reliance on Note Ons often creates repetitive, pattern-based music that leaves little room for nuance or expression. Everything that isn't dance music sounds like Philip Glass: It becomes non-physical, non-human music. (Yes, Glass is a successful composer, but if your only goal is to write like him, you don't need to read this article.)

It takes a traditional musician years to master a single instrument, to develop the ears, the micro-muscular responses, and the aesthetic sensitivity to make it produce music that others want to hear. Remember the first time you picked up a flute or a trumpet: Could you make any sound at all? The first time you pick up a new synth, it may sound great, but you are a long way from using its full capabilities.

The MIDI studio is, after all, a musical instrument. And like any other instrument, it needs to be mastered. Most of us don't give ourselves enough time to learn the equipment. Every synth, every *patch* on every synth, has a playing technique. A good patch should provide room for exploration and expression, but most of us just choose something quick and simple.

Samplers are particularly seductive. A sampler records the sound of a specific instrument playing a specific note in a specific way. Many users think that's all it takes to capture that instrument's essence. But to convincingly re-create a real instrument requires many samples, many ways to choose among them that make musical sense, and a playing (or sequencing) technique that reflects an understanding of how the instrument is played.

Proper use of velocity, aftertouch, and mod wheel *can* effectively simulate a real violin performance. But if you don't know exactly what a violin sounds like, you won't fool anybody.

MIXING

Because the technology gives MIDI users a rich vocabulary and great control over so many aspects of their music, many start to believe they can handle the composing, arranging, mixing, recording, and editing all by themselves, with equal facility. MIDI is empowering, but it's not magic. Let's face it, most of us can't deal with all that. I've been mixing music for nearly twenty years, but when I have an important project, I still hire a mixing engineer.

A lousy mix can be a dead giveaway of what would otherwise be an acceptable MIDI-produced track. In an acoustic session, an engineer would never spread out a piano so it takes up the entire stereo image and then put a five-piece horn section in mono, dead center. But an inexperienced MIDI musician, equipped with a brass patch

on a one-output synth and a stereo piano sample, might do just that.

Onboard processing, while it can make a synth sound much better in the store, can get you into trouble in a mix. A half-dozen synths mixed together, each with its own peculiar reverb, often results in a mishmash of unrelated acoustic spaces that sound unreal and out of control.

The other side of the coin is that MIDI makes it *too* easy to sound good. In the past, a killer piano sound required a quality piano, mics, room, and engineer. Today all you need is a $500 box. Good-sounding instruments make even bad music sound decent to the non-discerning ear.

HARDWARE LIMITATIONS

Before you start believing it's all your fault, rest assured that manufacturers share the blame. Few manufacturers produce anything that challenges the MIDI status quo. Wonderful new products come out all the time, but few offer any radical new ways to exploit MIDI. And those that do are difficult to find because nobody knows how to support or sell them. Occasionally a major manufacturer dares to create something truly revolutionary. But unless it's an overnight smash, the manufacturer usually gives up on the product before it has a chance to take hold.

Here's an example: An important characteristic of string and wind instruments is that the speed and depth of vibrato are independent of each other. In the vast majority of digital synths, however, a patch's low-frequency oscillation (LFO) or vibrato speed is fixed. Even if your synth lets you control speed and depth separately (like the Kurzweil 1000 series and Oberheim's Matrixes), you've probably never tried to set up a patch that takes advantage of this capability. This isn't because you're dumb; it's because the manufacturer has buried it in the software, not bothered to explain it in the manual, and failed to provide any presets that illustrate it.

Another example: Real singers and wind players can only produce one note at a time, but they get from one note to the next in a variety of ways, like sliding, breathing, or tonguing. Most synths have a switch for "mono" mode, but few actually behave any differently or offer any useful choice of articulations when they are in this mode. A "legato" controller is in the final stages of being written into the MIDI specification, but it fails to dictate how instruments will behave in legato mode; each manufacturer must take its own initiative on that front.

In fact, of the many useful additions to the MIDI spec in the last few years, few—except for MIDI Time Code and MIDI Sample Dump—have become common practice. Instruments that use general-purpose controllers or registered and non-registered parameters are still quite rare. Controller matrices finally are appearing in synthesizers, samplers, and effects processors, but few of these devices include factory patches with complex controller maps.

You could argue that constant technological innovation actually *harms* MIDI music. Many users feel pressured to have the latest, hippest noisemakers, and they never get a chance to fully explore a new toy before they move on to the next one.

SOFTWARE INTIMIDATION

Sequencer manufacturers often throw in new features without carefully considering how they will be used. A modern computer-based sequencer must delicately balance comprehensiveness and accessibility, or it will stifle the user's creative flow. For example, if you have to wade through all of a program's features to use its basic functions, you'll probably become frustrated and give up altogether.

At the same time, many programs still lack functions that could improve the realism of sequenced music enormously. For example, you should be able to tell a track to rush or drag *progressively* over a period of time, as a real instrumentalist often is asked to do.

Truly useful System Exclusive capabilities are also long overdue. Many sequencers offer SysEx recording and playback, so a synthesizer (or even a whole studio) can be reprogrammed at the beginning of every sequence, but this could go further. Some synths only reach their full expressive capabilities when controlled by SysEx. To exploit this, sequencers need to give the user a chance to edit SysEx data like text and then send it within a sequence like any other MIDI event.

WHAT CAN YOU DO?

Despite our film-composer friend's experience, there *are* people out there creating great music with MIDI. Here are some things you can do to make sure you're in that group:

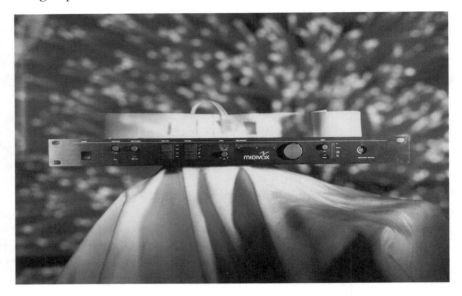

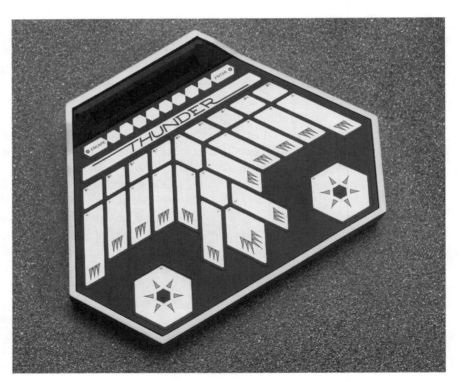

• Master your instrument. Take time to learn what your studio can do, and get good at doing it. Try to avoid spending all your time looking for the latest and coolest hardware; work with what you've got. As one successful but frustrated composer told me, "I've got all the tools I ever

Alternative controllers can help make MIDI-generated music more expressive. Buchla and Associates' Thunder (below) provides a unique control surface for human hands which is completely different from a traditional piano keyboard. SynchroVoice's MIDIVox (above) enables skilled vocalists to convert singing into MIDI messages.

wanted. Now I wish they'd just leave me alone and let me make music!" Maybe you can get the complex sound you want by layering two instruments or using processing, instead of searching for that one synth you think will do it all for you.

For a good exercise, try working with classical pieces and see if you can make them sound convincing on your equipment. It doesn't matter if you don't have a string sampler. You don't need a specific acoustic sound to make an orchestral point. Instead, you can use something that fulfills the same function as that sound and make it come alive under its *own* terms. For example, where an orchestral composer would use a viola section to fill in a chord, you might get the same effect with a vocal pad. While it won't sound exactly the same, it might fit well with the rest of the sounds you use.

- Learn how to make music breathe. Sometimes it helps to think of each instrument as a human voice and shape each line as if you were singing it. Whether you're imitating an instrument or creating something entirely new, imagine how that instrument *feels* to play, and figure out how to translate that into finger and controller movements.

- Learn about orchestration (see "Electronic Orchestration," p. 79). The principles of orchestrating for electronic instruments are largely the same as for acoustic instruments: Different timbres should complement each other and stay out one another's way. Make sure each line has its own distinct spectral space. Keep things from getting muddy. Learn about mixing; it goes hand in hand with orchestration. Learn how to create spaces with processing and how to keep elements distinct, even as they blend.

- Try alternative controllers. Get a couple of MIDI drum pads, or try a MIDI guitar. Even the lousiest MIDI guitar does note and chord combinations that are clumsy to play on a keyboard. If you sing, spend some time with a pitch-to-MIDI converter. If you play woodwinds—even a penny whistle or a recorder—try a MIDI wind controller. Even at the simplest level, these can add new layers of expressiveness to your music. And if you really get

into it, you can create a unique compositional voice for yourself.

If you can devote time to them, look at the truly alternative controllers from Don Buchla or alternative composition programs like *M* or *Music Mouse*. Try to expand your vocabulary beyond the Note On/Note Off totalitarianism of keyboards.

- Get out of the studio once in a while. Go out and listen to some real music: not Milli Vanilli, but chamber music, jazz, or ethnic music. Hear how these performers use subtle changes in time, pitch, timbre, and vibrato to make their expressive points. Think about how you can adopt some of those techniques to your music.

- Collaborate. MIDI is making one-man bands out of many people, but not all of us are up to the gig. Even if you have the best instrumental, orchestration, and engineering chops in the world, you can gain perspective by working—playing, programming, or mixing—with someone with a different perspective.

CAN WE DO THIS?

I believe in MIDI. I have spent the past eight years immersed in it, and it has changed my life in more ways than I can count. I intend to keep working with it for a long time. Needless to say, it drives me nuts to hear "It isn't good enough," or "It isn't pro," or "I want *real* music."

We, as users and developers, have not done all we can to realize MIDI's potential. But it's not from lack of desire. We all (well, most of us) live in the real world and are constrained by real-world economics. Manufacturers have to sell to fickle customers, compete in a highly fashion-conscious market, and constantly introduce new products to stay competitive. Users must justify the costs of their equipment, meet client schedules, and feed, house, and clothe themselves and their families. Few of us on either side of the equation have unlimited time to experiment, to play, to continuously seek out new forms of creative expression.

But unless that precise form of play is encouraged, and unless MIDI demonstrates its creative—not just commercial—potential, it will always be associated with "machine music." And that will be a great loss to humans. ♪

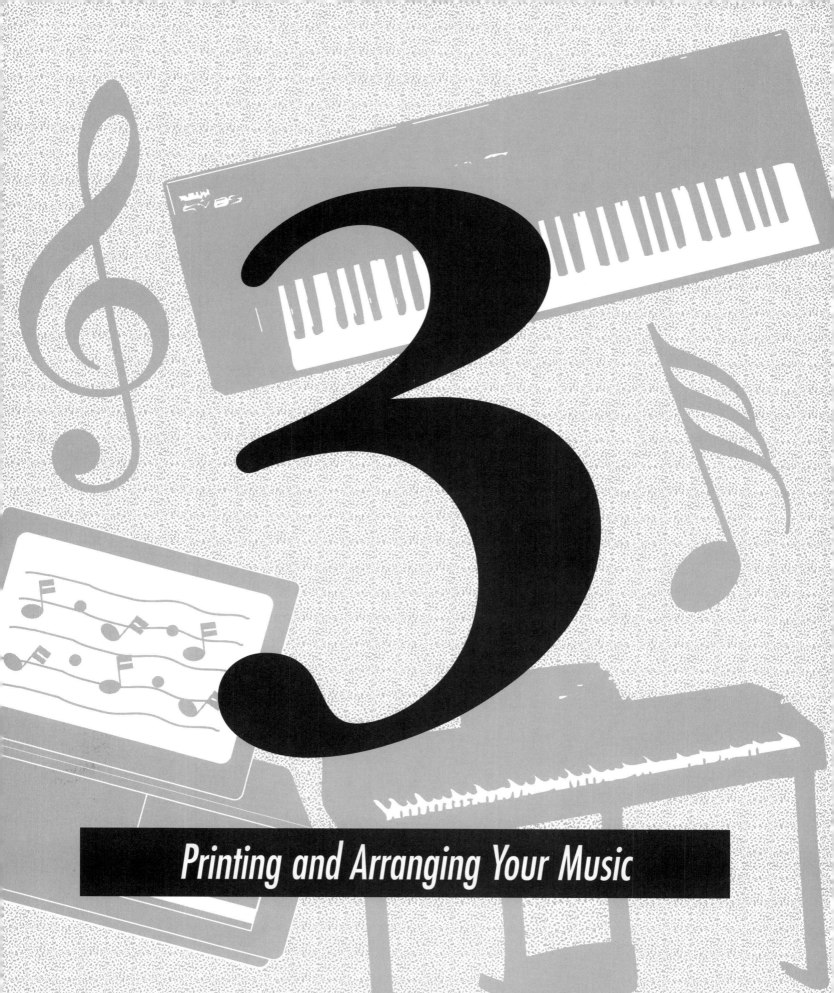

3

Printing and Arranging Your Music

Choosing Musical Notation Software

More than 600 years have gone into the development of conventional music notation. Despite this fact, music software developers initially excluded conventional notation as a means of representing musical data for computers and attempted to foist new systems, such as alphanumeric event lists and "piano roll" bar graphs, in its place.

However, it's not easy to ignore six centuries of musical language. Music publishers and engravers, copyists, orchestrators, arrangers, and performers do not communicate via printed event lists and bar graphs. The development of music notation software marries the computer's unlimited editing power to the symbols that preserve music through the ages.

There are many good arguments for pursuing music notation by computer. Due to repetition and modified repetition, cutting and pasting easily arranges musical information that is reusable within the same piece. Automatic proofreading of parameters such as rhythm and instrumental range is simplified by the computer, and interactive "proofhearing" and ease of editing are obvious advantages for composers and orchestrators. In the music-publishing industry, computers make it possible for several people to work on the same job. A well-devised notation program can substitute for manual dexterity and, to a certain extent, musical knowledge.

The development of music notation software was stimulated by the introduction of Adobe Systems' printer-independent Post-Script music font, "Sonata," designed by Cleo Huggins in 1986. Amazingly, no standardized, computer-based musical symbol set existed until the release of the Adobe font. Today, over two dozen PostScript music fonts are available for creating professional-looking music.

BY
**CHRISTOPHER
YAVELOW**

WHY NOTATION SOFTWARE?

There are two fundamental reasons for using music notation software: the manipulation of preexisting music and the creation of new music. The first category includes publishing, engraving, copying, arranging, and orchestration. The second category includes composition and musical realization.

Notation software performs a variety of tasks: (1) Production of a final legible copy for publication or distribution; (2) Extraction of parts required for performance; (3) Creation of new versions of existing works in different keys; (4) Rapid creation of a new arrangement via software tools; (5) Easy musical idea manipulation via software tools; (6) Creation of an electronic realization as an instant reference

"Polaroid" (as they say in Hollywood), or for "proofhearing"; and (7) Creation of an electronic realization as an end in itself. The order of this list is not arbitrary. It progresses from tasks concerned primarily with form (the graphical elements, or "look") to those concerned with content (the musical interpretation of symbols).

To assist you in choosing a notation package, this article lists some of the more important features to consider when evaluating different programs. Be wary of simply picking the program with the most features (unless you happen to be an engraver). In most cases, the more features a program has, the harder it is to master and the slower it runs. Also, don't pay for features you'll never use. Determine what you need in a notation program and purchase accordingly.

SYSTEM REQUIREMENTS
There is an absolute minimum horsepower needed to run any piece of software. Remember that it is in the manufacturer's interest to state that their program runs on an inexpensive system, even if it takes ten minutes to copy four bars of music. Try the software on the computer you plan to use, and bring a stopwatch.

Beware of companies' claims that a hard disk is not required. Notation files are often ten to 100 times larger than MIDI sequencer files of the same data. While a single-page lead sheet may be generated with a floppy drive-based system, larger files require a hard disk.

VIEWING MODES
Some programs provide for viewing and editing music as if it were a virtual *page* on the computer screen. Other programs take the *scroll* approach: The music appears on one continuous staff that might be 20 or 30 feet long in the real world. The more elegant programs allow switching between page view and scroll view, with no restrictions on editing in either domain.

MAXIMUM NUMBER OF STAVES
There is a correlation between price and the number of staves a program supports, so determining your needs is important. Notating symphonies requires more than eight staves, but seldom more than 32.

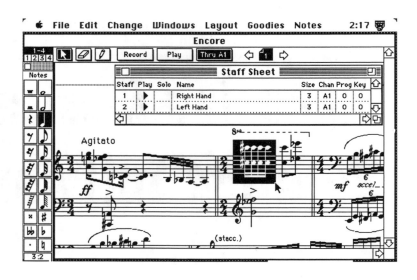

Encore's (by Passport) main window showing music with an area selected for editing, along with the palette showing notes and rests and the staff sheet.

However, if notation software is used to drive synthesizers, one stave for each of the sixteen MIDI channels is necessary. If your MIDI interface supports multiple channels, you may want as many as 64 staves.

USER PREFERENCES
Many professional engravers have cultivated a style to the extent that a single manuscript page is easily identified as, for example, a Hal Leonard, Schirmer, or Henle edition. Some programs permit user customization by allowing adjustment of variables such as beam angle and thickness, dot offset, and stem width. This sort of control adds a good deal to the price and many kilobytes to the size of a notation program.

In many ways, a music notation program functions like page-layout software; as with these packages, it's important to have complete positioning control over each of the elements that make up a page. The ability to move individual elements such as expression marks, accidentals, and beams often makes the difference between professional-looking music and not-quite-professional results.

RHYTHMIC RESOLUTION
The available symbol set is extremely important. If the program doesn't allow 128th notes, and you suddenly need to write one, you're out of luck. Be sure to determine the minimum note value the program can generate.

OPTIONAL NOTEHEADS

Having the option of using diamond noteheads is important if you're notating string harmonics. Likewise, guitar notation may require slashes and percussion transcription X's. If you include cues in your score, you need the ability to intermingle notehead sizes on the same staff. This is another area where it is important to ensure a program meets your needs.

CLEFS

Clefs are yet another individual case. Chopin composed most of his *oeuvre* using treble (G) and bass (F) clefs exclusively.

MIXED KEY SIGNATURES

Most notation programs support standard circle-of-fifths key signatures. But if you need to mix sharps and flats in a signature, make sure the software allows it. Also, if you change keys mid-song, not every program provides for signature cancellations. On those that do, a bank including natural signs indicates which accidentals in the previous key are no longer in effect.

COMPLEX METERS

Most programs provide for standard time signatures. If complex (2 + 4/8), fractional (3.5/4), or multiple (having different numbers of beats but with coinciding barlines) meter signatures are characteristic of your musical language, software options are limited. Provisions for alternating signatures (6/8 + 3/4) such as Leonard Bernstein used in "America" are almost non-existent, but there are obvious work-arounds if the software allows them (change the meter signature at every bar, or use triplets).

CHORD SYMBOLS

Many programs now offer the option of placing chord symbols over staves. Some offer text symbols only, others provide fretboard notation, and some allow both. The best implementation of chord symbols automatically transposes them when the music is transposed to a new key. Some programs allow specification of a unique MIDI channel for chord symbols to play back on, complete with voicing options. If your software lacks a chord-symbol option, you sometimes can get around this by creating a lyric line above the staff and using one of the available chord-symbol fonts.

CROSS-STAFF BEAMING

Diagonal beaming is now the standard for notation programs, so don't settle for anything less. For notating complex keyboard music, however, you also should look for beams that can cross staves.

TUPLET RANGE

Notation programmers often labor under the false assumption that no one needs to notate any tuplet greater than a triplet. Some provide for triplets, and quintuplets at best.

MUSIC INPUT

Fast and efficient data entry is the most difficult and important task notation programs fulfill. In many cases, you'll spend more time entering the music than anything else, so it's important to make the

Dr. T's *The Copyist* Postscript printout

process easy and offer as many choices as possible. Many programs use MIDI as their main form of input, but the type of MIDI implementation varies widely.

Real-time MIDI entry, which allows you to simply play as if into a sequencer, is not a trivial programming feat. You should worship the programmers if your software can accomplish this. From a programmer's standpoint, real-time entry is easiest if the software supplies a metronome click to play to.

Step-time MIDI entry refers to specifying a note duration by way of computer keyboard or mouse, then playing the note or chord on a MIDI keyboard to specify pitch. One feature to look for with step-time entry is the ability to "lock in" a duration. With this feature, if you need to enter 100 sixteenth notes in a row, you don't have to manually specify the duration before you play each note.

Importing Standard MIDI Files is an important feature for a notation program if you are involved in MIDI sequencing. You may have hundreds of completed sequences you want printed in notation, and a program's ability to import Standard MIDI Files and convert them to notation saves endless data reentry. And if you want to share your work with someone owning a different notation program, or you want to do more work with the MIDI data in your favorite sequencer, the ability to export Standard MIDI Files is essential.

Most non-MIDI input strategies are some variation on the theme of selecting a rhythmic value from an onscreen palette or specifying a duration with the computer keyboard and then clicking the note at its desired location with a mouse. Some systems turn the computer keyboard into a veritable musical keyboard by remapping the keys, while others position notes with cursor arrows instead of a mouse.

TEXT INPUT

The degree of lyric input flexibility you require involves determining how many verses you normally need and whether fonts should be mixed (most foreign language translations are in italics beneath the non-italicized original lyric). Another important feature is the ability to "bind" syllables to notes, so that reformatting a piece of music automatically reformats the lyrics as well.

You may require text beyond lyrics. A good example is stage directions in an operatic work. Make sure it is possible to "attach" text to particular measures, staves, or systems so that reformatting your music moves the annotative text along with the specific music it relates to. Other text you may require includes such automatically placed items as headers, footers, and page numbers.

POSTSCRIPT

An important consideration is whether the notation software prints PostScript. PostScript, a page-description language developed by Adobe Systems, offers many

advantages. The main benefit is printer independence. Any printer that understands PostScript can print your files at its highest resolution. Other advantages include a wealth of PostScript music fonts (32 and counting) and the capability to scale output to any possible reduction or enlargement. TrueType is a type system developed by Apple and Microsoft that offers many of the same benefits for both Macintosh and IBM computers. Some PC programs offer high-resolution output on non-PostScript laser printers.

TRANSPOSITION

The option to transpose music is important for two reasons. First, you may wish to print out music in a different key to accommodate the vocal range of a singer. Second, some instances of repeated musical phrases within a piece may warrant a new transposition. There are many ways material can be transposed: chromatically, diatonically, enharmonically, modally, or by user-defined scale. Such custom pitch-remapping allows, among other things, rapid changing of a passage from major to minor or Lydian mode. An easy way to check if the software transposes correctly is to move a passage from the key of C to C#. The third and seventh degrees of the scale should renotate at B# and E# accordingly, *not* C and F natural.

PART EXTRACTION

If you need orchestral parts on a regular basis, examine part-extraction capabilities carefully. The best implementation is for the software to create separate parts files automatically. This allows you to go in and tweak them if necessary (to assure page turns are humanly possible, etc.). Some programs create parts directly from the score file without allowing any control over formatting. This is fine if the program does it correctly, but most don't. Instrumental parts usually "concatenate" groups of rests into one long, multi-measure rest with a large number over it. The software should be intelligent enough to break these multi-measure rests at tempo, meter, and key changes, as well as other places you indicate in the master score.

Two useful features are the automatic placement of the instrument's name in the upper left corner of the part (where it be-

longs) and the ability to auto-reformat parts as they are output, whether to a file or directly to the printer. The notes in instrumental parts are expected to be tightly spaced to require as few page turns as possible. The program should take care of this for you.

MIDI CHANNELS PER STAVE

The ability to assign separate MIDI channels to staves—and even separate voices on the same stave—turns your notation software into a veritable MIDI sequencer and facilitates proofhearing your masterpiece. The option to initialize each staff with a patch-change message saves a great deal of setup time during playback of notation files. Having the music scroll by during playback often is regarded as a courtesy feature, but it actually is quite important. When listening to a piece of music without a computer, you probably flip score pages as the playback progresses. It helps when the computer does this for you onscreen, because it never gets lost.

MIDI EXPRESSION MARKS

Programs with the most sophisticated MIDI implementation include the ability to assign MIDI messages that affect playback to expression marks. For example, a ritard on the page can slow down the rate of MIDI clocks, or a forte can affect the velocity level of notes being played. Those

who want an accurate playback of what they write will find this feature invaluable.

MIDI EDITING

If you intend to use your notation software as a sequencer (and not just for simple proofhearing), it should provide some of the MIDI data-editing features offered by dedicated MIDI sequencers. Don't assume because a program allows MIDI input that it retains velocity, controller, or tempo data. Most limit MIDI data capture to pitch. Others capture all associated MIDI data but don't allow editing.

THE BOTTOM LINE

Music publishers often invest five-figure sums in the engraving, printing, and distribution of each musical composition they publish. Many current notation packages are well on their way to eliminating these expenses. Soon, publishers may stop weighing the odds of recovering their investment in a publication: They will be able to store all of their works on a disk and print them as the need arises. Furthermore, it is increasingly common for a composer to supply music already notated on disk, which represents further savings for publishers. As more notation files of musical works are distributed via telecommunications, the long-awaited concept of "publication on demand" may become a reality. ♪

71

Choosing a Printer for Music Notation

BY
DAVID (RUDY)
TRUBITT

It's a big mistake to select your notation program and printer independently when they need to work as a team. Many factors go into choosing a music notation program, but one that's not so obvious is the method of communication between computer and printer. You'll find it easier to select and use your score-printing tools when you have a basic understanding of how notation data onscreen becomes graphical data on the printed page.

The computer screen (or a television screen) displays objects as a collection of tiny dots. The conversion from the geometric shapes that software programs work with internally into the dots (also called bits, pixels, points, etc.) you see on the computer screen is called *rasterization*. A collection of these dots is called a *bitmap*. The rasterization process could be considered a visual analogy to the sampling of audio waveforms. Images must be rasterized to be shown onscreen.

Similarly, data (such as notation) you wish to print must be rasterized so that dot-matrix, inkjet, and laser printers can produce the series of small dots we see as graphics. On the Macintosh, QuickDraw is used to communicate both to the screen and to non-PostScript printers such as the Apple ImageWriter. PCs have no common format, so various software drivers are used, depending on hardware configuration. In the world of notation, there are two primary ways to print graphical information: describing the page as a bitmap (dots on a field of white-space) and Adobe Systems' PostScript (discussed later), a language that describes objects on a page in geometric terms (such as lines and arcs).

For both displays and printers, using a higher number of smaller dots produces a clearer, sharper picture. This characteristic, called *resolution*, is measured in dots per inch (dpi). An inkjet or laser printer can achieve 300 dpi or more, while less-expensive dot-matrix printers might print at half that. The resolution of video displays is usually much lower than that of printers (e.g., 72 dpi for a standard Mac display), so the rasterization process is normally performed separately for each. Keep in mind that even the best printer can't print your score at its maximum capability unless your notation program supports its high-resolution features.

In **Fig. 3.1**, the quarter note on the left is shown at two different resolutions. The image on the right is rasterized with a resolution twice that of the center example. Note that a doubling of dots per inch causes a four-fold increase in total number of dots. Although vertical lines are pretty clean in both cases, approximation of curved shapes improves the most from increased resolution. There are plenty of curves and angled lines in music notation (clefs, noteheads, etc.), so a high-resolution printer makes a big difference.

FUN WITH FONTS

Fonts are another important concept to grasp. A font is a group of graphic symbols (typically resembling the alphanumeric characters in a particular typeface, such as Helvetica or Times Roman), one of which corresponds to each of the 256 possible keys and special key combinations on the keyboard (the ASCII character set).

Some fonts contain symbols other than alphanumeric characters. Adobe developed a font called "Sonata" that contains music notation symbols. Instead of printing the letter "q," the Sonata font prints a quarter note; instead of "h," it produces a half note, and so on. Some notation packages come with their own fonts rather than using Sonata; for instance, Coda's *Finale* and *MusicProse* notation programs use their own fonts, "Petrucci" and "Seville." *Finale* uses additional fonts for musical symbols, including a font of MIDI symbols. If you're interested, there are programs such as Altsys' *Fontographer* which let you modify or create your own bit-mapped and PostScript fonts.

BIT-MAPPED PRINTERS

As mentioned before, there are two basic ways of printing music notation and correspondingly, two types of printers. Those that require the *computer* to perform the rasterization process and transmit the resulting bitmap are called bit-mapped printers. These bit-mapped models are less expensive than PostScript-compatible devices (discussed later), and many of them offer high-quality output.

Most dot-matrix printers (which are by definition bit-mapped devices) are compatible with the Epson printer format, which is supported by many notation programs. If you're considering a dot-matrix printer, especially for an IBM PC system, Epson compatibility is a big plus. Alternately, Hewlett-Packard's DeskJet and LaserJet printers require bit maps in their own non-Epson format. Because of their popularity and high-quality output, many software vendors also have written additional software drivers to support these devices. A company developing a new printer must support the Epson format or the less-common HP format, or convince software vendors that special support for

their product is warranted. Even within the Epson product line, there are printers sporting features not supported by other models, making the Epson "format" a bit more like a guideline. Contact the notation program's manufacturer to be sure their program supports the printer you plan to use.

There are some drawbacks to transferring bitmaps from computer to printer. It can be more difficult for software vendors to scale (enlarge or reduce) notation symbols when sending bit-mapped data to printers. Bit-mapped fonts come in specific type sizes (e.g., 9-point, 12-point, 18-point, etc.), and if you want to use a size you don't have, you have to "fake it" by scaling the sizes you do have. Unfortunately, bitmaps distort when enlarged or reduced—the more they're scaled, the more jagged they look—so it's best to load fonts into your system in each point size you want to use (unless you have access to outline fonts, which can be expanded and contracted without distortion).

In addition, the amount of data contained in a single page of bit-mapped graphics can exceed millions of bits. Normally, this data is not stored all at once on your disk, but is sent to the printer as it is generated. This is a disadvantage if your printer is not wired directly to your computer. For example, say you have a cheap dot-matrix at home to print draft copies and a laser printer at work. The only way to get a final copy on the laser printer of notation prepared at home is by installing your notation package on your work computer—probably violating the terms of your software license—and reprinting the score from the notation file. The amount of data involved (to say nothing of the possibility of printer incompatibility) would prevent you from simply saving the page's bitmap to a floppy disk and later dumping it to the laser printer. However, this is not a problem when using PostScript.

POSTSCRIPT

Adobe Systems describes their PostScript format as a page-description language. Instead of using a set of dots (as with a bit-mapped font), a PostScript font includes a set of commands, stored as a text file, that mathematically describe the lines and curves that make up each character in the

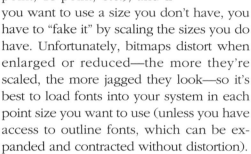

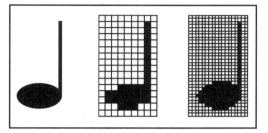

Figure 3.1 The quarter note on the left is shown at two different resolutions. The image on the right is rasterized with a resolution twice that of the center example.

typeface. (Bit-mapped images can be contained in a PostScript file as well.) PostScript printers must have the processing power to rasterize the description by themselves, as opposed to letting the computer do the job. This built-in computing ability (and the license fee manufacturers must pay to Adobe) make PostScript printers significantly more expensive than their bit-mapped counterparts.

When the computer transmits an ASCII symbol (an alphanumeric character, musical note, etc.) to a PostScript printer, the printer pulls the corresponding symbol in the correct typeface from its memory, or downloads the data from the computer. The printer then scales the symbol, rasterizes it, and prints it. Although PostScript has commands for drawing geometric objects that could create notation without a dedicated music font, the use of fonts is far more efficient.

PostScript fonts are divided into two classes, Type 1 and Type 3. (Type 2 fonts were part of a technology that didn't work out.) Type 1 fonts, such as Adobe's Sonata and Coda's Petrucci and Seville, are encrypted and contain scaling algorithms called *hints* that improve their appearance when rasterized at small sizes. Type 3 fonts are unencrypted fonts without hints and aren't as sharp at low resolution as Type 1 fonts (the effect is mostly noticeable in small sizes). With high-resolution printers, where the dots in the grid are smaller and there are more dots per inch, the two types are closer in quality.

In contrast with bit-mapped printers, writing PostScript commands to a disk file (using a Print to File command) instead of sending them directly to a printer can give you some extra flexibility. The file, with your fonts but without the notation software, could be printed by a PostScript device not attached to your computer. You could also send it over a modem, but PostScript files can get pretty big, too. Many self-serve copy shops offer access to PostScript laser printers (like the Apple LaserWriter), and there are typesetting shops that can take PostScript files and print them on professional typesetting machines for resolution as high as 1,270 or 2,540 dpi.

While it's always nice to have the finest resolution possible, you will pay more for it. PostScript is probably the way to go for the highest-possible quality output, but unless you're preparing a score for publi-cation, resolution this high is excessive and expensive (at least $5 per page from service bureaus).

PostScript's biggest limitation is the cost of the printers themselves. Also, paper sizes larger than 8 $\frac{1}{2}$ by 14 inches are less common among PostScript printers and are even *more* expensive. Non-PostScript, wide-carriage, dot-matrix printers offer a much less expensive path to larger paper sizes, which can be convenient for full scores.

POSTSCRIPT CLONES

To complicate matters, several manufacturers offer printers that attempt to emulate PostScript printers. One issue with PostScript clones is their compatibility with Adobe's fonts. Most "clones" can't use encrypted, Type 1 fonts, so they utilize unencrypted fonts, with hints, from other companies. Now that Adobe has released the Type 1 specification, completely PostScript-compatible printers can be developed without licensing the technology from Adobe.

Another option if you want Postscript output is PostScript emulation programs, which can read PostScript files and fonts, rasterize them, and send them to non-PostScript printers. In this way, these printers can get some of the benefits of PostScript and its fonts. *Adobe Type Manager* (ATM), which is available on the Mac and PC, works for PostScript Type 1 fonts, while Custom Applications Inc.'s *Freedom of Press* (available for the Mac and PC) can do this for both fonts and PostScript drawing commands.

Another printing technology not yet mentioned is TrueType, which is conceptually very similar to PostScript. At this time, it appears that PostScript will probably prevail over TrueType in the marketplace.

P.S.

Try to find an appropriate level of quality for your needs. Are you preparing a score for publication, or handing out lead sheets to your band? Remember, you have a wide range of choices, from low-resolution, bit-mapped output to PostScript laser output. (For the finest copy, you can even use PostScript-compatible electronic typesetting machines such as Linotronic.) Select compatible notation programs and printers. Finally, try to keep these technical details from drowning out the creative aspect of your music. I'd take musical content over dots per inch every time. ♪

74

Using Notation Software

Every year or two, a ground-breaking notation package is introduced amid claims that it is faster, easier to use, and more powerful than any previously released program. And while those claims often are true (better packages *are* coming out all the time), a single notation program has yet to emerge that does for musicians what *Excel* has done for businesspeople or what *PageMaker* has done for desktop publishers.

While we wait for the ultimate package to appear, there are many ways to improve the utility of available programs. Here are a few tips to help you get more out of your current notation software.

STARTING FROM SCRATCH

Many people find themselves constantly writing for similar groups of instruments, so before you enter a single note, create templates for the ensembles with which you frequently work. In addition to obvious things like clefs and instrument names, include placeholders for titles, credits, copyright notices, and anything else you regularly use.

In a notation program, the order in which you do things makes a big difference. For example, don't bother tweaking the page layout before you enter the lyrics: Long words often require additional space between notes, which affects the layout of measures in a system. As a rule of thumb, enter notes first; go on to dynamic markings, articulation markings, and lyrics; and then take a shot at the layout.

This procedure works because many graphic objects must be positioned relative to other objects. If you move a note, any articulations, dynamics, slurs, or lyrics must move with it. Some programs are better at this than others. Most of them keep track of lyrics and articulations when notes are shifted, but many do not handle slurs intelligently.

BY
STEVE PEHA

MINIMIZING SCREEN REDRAW

A root canal is nothing compared to the torture some programs put you through every time they redraw the screen. Minimizing screen-redraw time is one of the most important productivity enhancements that notation software users can make.

For those of you with color monitors, try running in monochrome. Music notation is one of the few graphics-oriented applications that does not require color. Depending on your system's video performance, this alone may decrease screen-redraw time by as much as 25 to 50 percent. This is especially true for Mac users who rely on the built-in 8-bit video capabilities of machines like the IIsi and IIci. *Windows* users should look into some of the new, inexpensive, accelerated video cards.

Finally, some programs have functions that let you inhibit redrawing. In some cases, you can specify that certain items not get redrawn. If you're not entering or editing the lyrics, why should the program waste your time redrawing them?

DOING IT BY HAND

Sometimes the thought of carefully positioning dozens of slurs or hundreds of staccato dots with a mouse makes me reach for my #2 pencil. Notation programs are fast for some things but terribly slow for others. So why fight it? Try doing some things by hand, like putting in slurs or dynamic markings with a trusty writing implement.

A good division of labor might be to enter notes and lyrics, work with the layout until the spacing looks good, then print it out and do the rest with a pencil or a pen. However, any symbols that are not input into a score will not appear in extracted parts, nor will MIDI playback of scores be entirely accurate if your program's MIDI output is affected by non-note markings.

If you're using a relatively low-resolution dot-matrix printer, you might benefit from a little interaction with your nearest photocopier. Dot-matrix output can look like it came from a laser printer after it's reduced on a copier. Even a slight reduction to 90 or 95 percent makes a noticeable improvement. If possible, print the music at a slightly enlarged size and reduce the output back down to 100 percent. The more you reduce, the higher your effective resolution. Even 300-dpi laser printer output can be improved in this way.

Many people buy notation software with the dream of scoring their masterpiece and then having the computer print out a beautiful set of parts automatically. Unfortunately, full-featured part extraction usually is found only in the most expensive programs. If your program can't extract parts (or can't extract them very well), don't worry. You can do it yourself by deleting staves from the score and leaving only the part you want to print out. This isn't very elegant, but it usually works. Handle your transpositions manually, and if you need multi-measure rests, just leave a blank measure in the appropriate places and draw them in yourself.

PREPARING FOR TRANSCRIPTION

Anyone who has ever tried to import a Standard MIDI File into a notation program knows that the results often are less than ideal. In some cases, the transcription may be useless. However, usable results are possible if you spend a little time performing some simple edits in the sequencer first.

The key is understanding the aspects of transcription that cause problems for computer programs. Your software must figure out pitch, rhythm, duration, and the location of each note in time. Pitch and location are easy. Even the worst notation programs transcribe pitches correctly from MIDI note numbers and put the notes in the right order. Duration is a little harder because we often perform with subtle articulations that make it difficult to determine correct note values. Rhythm is the toughest because many styles of music are performed differently than they are notated.

If you find that your playing differs from the notation you're hoping to print out as a result of articulation and rhythm, you should alter the durations and rhythms in your sequence before transcribing it. For example, how many times have you transcribed a line of music and gotten something like this:

when what you really wanted was this:

or perhaps even this:

Sure, you're just shortening the notes to give the line a staccato articulation, but does your notation software understand? Probably not. So before you transcribe your sequence, try expanding your durations to their full value so that every note is *legato* (having no silence between adjacent notes in a musical line). Some sequencers have a command to do this globally for an entire track or song. Otherwise, play the notes in staccato passages with longer durations.

CREATIVE QUANTIZING

Even if you don't read music, you probably understand rhythm better than your computer does. Using some creative quantizing, you can coax your notation software into producing the results you're looking for.

Let me use a personal example. A couple of years ago, I sat down to transcribe some very complicated jazz piano performances. Using an appropriate quantization level, my notation software correctly transcribed the rhythms in about seven or eight out of every ten measures. Unfortunately, two or three out of ten measures were hopelessly mangled. If I changed the quantization setting to more accurately match the music in these measures, the measures that previously had been transcribed correctly came out wrong.

Finally, it occurred to me that I could duplicate the track I was trying to transcribe. By quantizing one copy with one rhythmic value and the other copy with another value, and importing both copies into my notation program, I could pull out the correct parts from each copy to create the best possible transcription.

Here's a highly simplified example of this technique:

The eight-note swing rhythms of jazz and some pop styles present a unique challenge. The goal is to take eighth notes that have been played with a triplet feel and notate them as though they were normal "straight" eighths. Few notation programs are sophisticated enough to handle something like this automatically, but by combining track-shifting with quantization in your sequencer, eighth notes can be notated correctly (see **Fig. 3.2**).

When people play eighth notes with swing, the second eighth note in each beat is played on the last third of the beat, as though it were an eighth-note triplet. Quantizing to eighth-note resolution straightens these eighths out by moving the second eighth note in each pair back to the middle of the beat. However, eighth-note quantization is quite coarse; large parts of your music might be ruined. In general, quantizing to sixteenth notes produces better overall results, but all the swung eighths end up as sixteenth notes on the last quarter of the beat.

To prevent this from happening, shift the entire track forward in time before you quantize so that quantizing to sixteenth-note resolution pulls the off-beat eighths to the middle of the beat and not to the last sixteenth note. If the off-beat eighth notes fall exactly on the last eighth-note triplet (or 66 percent into the beat), move the track forward about four or five percent of

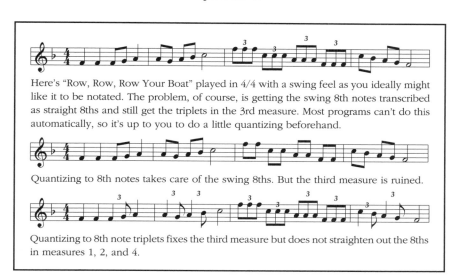

Here's "Row, Row, Row Your Boat" played in 4/4 with a swing feel as you ideally might like it to be notated. The problem, of course, is getting the swing 8th notes transcribed as straight 8ths and still get the triplets in the 3rd measure. Most programs can't do this automatically, so it's up to you to do a little quantizing beforehand.

Quantizing to 8th notes takes care of the swing 8ths. But the third measure is ruined.

Quantizing to 8th note triplets fixes the third measure but does not straighten out the 8ths in measures 1, 2, and 4.

one beat. That's about five clock ticks at 96 pulses per quarter notes (ppqn), or as many as 25 ticks at 480 ppqn. The more the music lays back (plays behind the beat), the more you'll need to shift the track to keep those off-beat eighth notes from becoming sixteenths.

OTHER CHALLENGES

Keyboard parts pose a bigger challenge to notation software than single-line instrumental parts. Even simple piano tracks often include multiple independent voices and other complexities that confuse the most savvy of notation programs.

The best thing to do is split the right and left hands onto separate tracks. If your sequencer has good graphic editing capabilities, this doesn't take long and saves you a lot of time in the long run. (If your music has hand crossovers, splitting hands won't work very well, but to be honest, crossovers are difficult to deal with anyway.) Once the hands are split, you may want to further separate any independent voices within the left- and right-hand parts. Transcribing multiple voices on one staff is almost impossible for a computer program to notate correctly.

Figure 3.2 By quantizing the same part two or more ways and then combining the results, you can usually get your sequences to notate properly.

Using Notation Software

No matter how incredible your notation program is or how much effort you expend editing a sequence prior to transcription, you'll probably never get exactly the kind of notation you want. There are two reasons for this problem. As we've seen, there often is a significant difference between the way something is played and the way it's notated. That difference has to do with style, and we can hardly expect today's personal computers to have a complete understanding of musical styles as they apply to transcription.

The second reason is that MIDI files don't contain information about important things like beaming, enharmonic accidentals, and articulations. So, even if the ultimate transcription program is introduced someday, you'll still have to correct a few sharps and flats, adjust the beaming, and put in your own articulation marks.

GRAPHIC MUSIC

It isn't enough just to know how to get your music into a notation program; you also need to know how to get it out. Moving your score into a word-processing or desktop-publishing environment usually is a matter of deciding which graphics file format to use. Most notation programs save their files in three graphic formats: EPS, TIFF, and bitmap.

The EPS (Encapsulated PostScript) format generally produces the best results. However, EPS files are large and slow to print, and require expensive laser printers to achieve the best results. You should use this format if you intend to print on a PostScript laser printer or high-resolution (1,200 to 2,400 dpi) PostScript imagesetter.

TIFF (Tag Image File Format) files also can be large and slow to print. Exporting TIFF files usually produces good results, although usually not as good as the EPS format. The primary advantage of TIFF files over EPS files is that they can be printed on less expensive non-PostScript printers without sacrificing quality.

The bitmap format is the simplest of all. It is low-resolution (generally 72 dpi), so the files are fairly small and easy to work with. Of course, the print quality is much lower than either TIFF or EPS. On the other hand, bitmap files can be imported or pasted into almost any word processor, graphics program, or DTP environment. If your notation program can't export graph-

ics in any known format, you can produce a bitmap file by taking a screen shot of the score. This works fine for small examples, but it's impractical for whole pages or entire scores.

LYRICS

Many notation programs allows you to import text from a word processor. I highly recommend that you take this approach if possible. Typing and editing text is much easier in a good word processor than it is in most notation programs (and don't forget about the benefits of spell-checking).

Some notation programs attach lyrics to notes automatically by looking for spaces in the middle of words and at their ends. Unlike regular writing, lyrics need hyphens inserted in every word that contains more than one syllable. Some word processors do this automatically if you ask them to display all discretionary hyphens in your text. If you can export your lyrics with all the hyphens intact, you can save yourself some tedious retyping. Even if your word processor can't do this automatically, you're probably better off doing the hyphenation in a word processor because you can check your word breaks against the word processor's hyphenation dictionary.

UPGRADING YOUR HARDWARE

It's easy to forget that notation programs are not really music programs at all; they're heavy-duty graphics and page-layout programs in disguise. On the Mac side, you should consider a fast 68030-equipped machine with 5 MB of RAM. With *Windows*, an 80386 machine running at 33 MHz with 4 MB of RAM is the minimum practical configuration.

Adding more RAM is the best way to improve performance on your existing computer.

A FINAL NOTE

It takes some ingenuity to get the most out of today's crop of music notation packages. But there is some good work being done by composers, arrangers, and publishers using off-the-shelf software. We're also starting to see software that can make rough transcriptions of a live performance instantly in real time. It won't be long before computers have the horsepower and programs have the smarts to produce good-looking notation just about as fast as you can play music in from a keyboard. ♩

Electronic Orchestration

BY
RENÉ SALM

A well-arranged composition is music to the ears. Average melodies can sound extraordinary when an optimum mix of musical elements is achieved, and good melodies seldom survive poor arrangements.

Navigating sonic landscapes is particularly dangerous for electronic musicians, due to the overwhelming number of options available. A collection of multitimbral synthesizers with built-in effects, combined with a powerful software sequencer, is an arrangement disaster waiting to happen.

The challenge for today's composer is to organize, manage, and control a wealth of resources. The best way to meet this challenge is to apply old-fashioned concepts of orchestration and arrangement. However, electronic music redefines the sound of the instrument and its projection into an acoustic space. Recognizing the impact of electronic instruments on basic orchestration principles is the first step to creating better compositions and arrangements.

WHAT'S ORCHESTRATION?

My musical dictionary defines orchestration as "the art of employing instruments in various combinations." This definition is quite clear in terms of acoustic ensembles, but the nature of electronic music makes it hard to define an electronic "instrument." A *patch* is the obvious answer, but it doesn't take into account expressive manipulation of an electronic sound through a controller, such as a keyboard or percussion pad.

An electronic instrument therefore must be defined as a patch *plus* the performance values of a particular controller. This fact enlarges the parameters of electronic instruments, because an identical sound played on a different controller becomes, in effect, a new sound. For example, a grand piano patch played by a keyboard controller assumes a completely different sonic quality when played by a MIDI wind controller. The orchestrator must account for this idiosyncracy of the electronic instrument when choosing tone colors for a particular arrangement.

The three basic elements distinguishing both acoustic and electronic sounds are pitch, amplitude, and timbre. Understanding how these three elements affect orchestration is essential for creating well-arranged music.

PITCH

One of the underlying principles of orchestration is that sounds compete with each other within the audio spectrum. Usually, if a trumpet and flute sound the same pitch, the flute is inaudible. But if the trumpet drops an octave or two, the flute emerges. Adding to the problem of competing instruments is a limited audio spectrum for musical instruments. For example, an 88-key piano ranges from 27 Hz to approximately 4,096 Hz (four octaves above middle C). In contrast, even the average 60-year-old can hear up to 8,000 Hz, and a young person's range peaks around 16,000 Hz.

In addition, most musically useful sounds have fairly complex overtones which, when combined with other sounds, diminish clarity. When a note is played on the piano, one pitch is perceived, but that pitch's many overtones give the sound its timbre. It's easy to overload regions of the audio spectrum if pitches and patches are indiscriminately piled upon each other. This temptation is increased by the growing polyphonic and multitimbral capabilities of today's instruments.

Orchestrators must assign sounds to discrete areas of the audio spectrum where they can maintain proper dispersion and clarity. To accomplish this, keep in mind the three basic regions of the spectrum: treble, midrange, and bass. This principle suggests an axiom of orchestration: A full and balanced effect requires that all three regions of the audio spectrum sound at once.

AMPLITUDE

Although a literal definition of amplitude is *loudness*, orchestrators are more concerned with "perceived loudness," which is relative. Listening to music at high decibel levels for an extended period acclimates the ears to the loudness until the volume is (relatively) comfortable. If a soft passage suddenly appears, an audience may barely notice it. The contrary also is true: A long, soft performance followed by an abrupt volume increase may leave an audience feeling as if their eardrums have exploded. It's the orchestrator's responsibility to balance perceived loudness and softness to achieve the optimum musical effect.

There are several ways to increase perceived loudness without increasing volume. Raising the pitch or shortening a sound's attack are two effective methods.

Also, limiters and compressors make a sound seem louder by decreasing the volume of its highest transients. The main body of the sound is proportionally louder and often cuts through a thick instrumental mix.

Using amplitude effectively in orchestration requires enough dynamic range to permit an ideal contrast between loud and soft, as well as intermediate volume levels. A symphony orchestra in a well-designed acoustic space posts a phenomenal range of approximately 70 decibels between its loudest and softest sounds. Synthesists must seek to maximize dynamic range relative to the listener.

The human ear's sensitivity to amplitude is greatest within a frequency range of 1,000 to 4,000 Hz (roughly the top two octaves of a piano). Within this fairly high range, the human ear can perceive incredibly faint tones. Sensitivity falls off progressively for lower tones and more rapidly for higher ones. Remember when you score for the treble region that this area needs little power to grab a listener's attention.

Another effect concerning amplitude is the phenomenon known as *masking*, where a loud tone obscures a softer one occurring at or near the same pitch. The effect is more apparent on soft, higher-pitched tones; thus, masking is more pronounced in the bass region, where overtones are the strongest. Because of this, loud bass notes require lots of vertical space in an arrangement. (Vertical space refers to the intervals between notes in a chord.)

An old principle of classical orchestration is to distribute the sounds of a chord according to the harmonic series, with the widest spaces toward the bass end. This particular distribution produces a full, blended sound as the various fundamentals and their overtones reinforce each other. In this case, masking is avoided through the judicious choice of amplitude levels and timbres.

TIMBRE

My trusty dictionary defines timbre as "the character of a sound, as distinct from its pitch; hence the quality of sound that distinguishes one instrument from another."

The perception of character requires attention to a sound's attack, envelope, and overtone structure.

Timbre is especially important in orchestration because an instrument's character prompts you to include it in an arrangement. Another basic principle of orchestration is maintaining interest through contrasting timbres, such as thin sounds against thick, fast attacks against slow, and bright sounds against dark.

Unlike pitch or amplitude, timbre is a subjective term. The lack of an objective measurement forces the orchestrator to break down the qualities of sound to facilitate the definition and placement of timbres in the work.

• **Attack** Sounds are easily contrasted on the basis of a short attack (percussive, plucked, explosive) or long attack (any type of sound with an initial rising amplitude envelope). Human ears are highly discriminating in this respect; a minute difference between the attack speeds of two sounds renders an effective contrast.

Human ears are so sharp that attack transients (brief, non-sustaining overtones) occurring in the first few milliseconds of a sound are critical to our perception of that sound. **Fig. 3.3** shows a graphic representation of the enormously complex attack portion of a violin tone, representing the bow's bite into the string.

Electronic instruments create contrasting timbres by attaching varied and complex attacks to longer sustaining sounds. Sampling technology made this easy, and many manufacturers use the concept as the basis for their instrument's sound-generating technology.

• **Thickness** Timbres also can be contrasted on the basis of those with many overtones (thick, rich, colorful) and those with few overtones (thin, clear). Examples of thick timbres are gongs, timpani, and cymbals. The flute is a classic thin timbre.

A thick timbre also must include some element of sustain. A complex set of overtones with a short duration won't survive the attack portion of the sound; it produces instead a dry, distinctive timbre like a wood block or marimba.

A thin timbre has relatively few overtones. These "transparent" timbres are use-

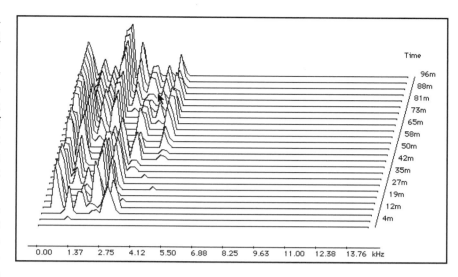

ful when clarity of sound is important. Thin timbres don't have to contrast directly with thick ones. In fact, such opposition is rather lopsided. A more musical-sounding result is attained when two or more thin timbres are combined. This method also works for building thick timbres, as it adds maximum flexibility to your sounds. Simply break down thicker sounds into two or

Figure 3.3 A harmonic analysis of the attack of a violin tone, showing the first few harmonics. Notice how each harmonic has amplitude envelopes far more complex than typical ADSRs.

MIDI CONTROLLERS

As part of the language of MIDI, electronic orchestrators have a number of controllers at their disposal. It is important to understand their relationship to acoustical counterparts. Topping the list are Velocity, Pressure, and Volume. Synth programmers often assign overall volume (not to be confused with MIDI controller 7) as an attribute of velocity. In other words, the speed at which a key is pressed determines how loud it is. However, in some cases it is more effective to use pressure to control the dynamics of a passage. Velocity works better to adjust a sound's attack, and many synths and samplers allow you to create this modulation routing. You also can experiment with velocity switching. For example, if you have two synths, one with a good slow brass and another with a good attack brass, you can assign them to the same MIDI channel and adjust the velocity cutoff of each.

It's also a good idea to distinguish between MIDI Volume (controller 7) and the dynamics generated with velocity. Use MIDI Volume initially to balance each instrument and create overall level adjustments and velocity (or pressure, if you've programmed a sound that way) to bring out particular notes. In other words, MIDI Volume should cover general dynamic markings and velocity should provide individual accents. You also can use MIDI-programmed EQs to add emphasis to certain notes or instruments. Every orchestral instrument has an acoustical foundation or fundamental tone that sets up the overtone content; EQing for that pitch and its subsequent overtones adds a great deal of realism to a synth. —*Ron Reaser* more thinner components and use them as building blocks.

• Pitched vs. Unpitched Pitch may be considered a parameter of timbre, as pitch depends on a certain regularity in the overtone structure. Also, note that many unpitched sounds actually possess some sense of pitch. The howling of wind reveals a fundamental that appears and disappears, sometimes moving higher, sometimes lower. Therefore, unpitched sounds can be layered with pitched ones to evoke timbre thickness, color, or atmospheric effect. An unpitched timbre with a short or definite attack (a drum, etc.) gives a pitched sound rhythmic definition and percussiveness. A truly unpitched sound often has a formant (a sharp amplitude peak in the frequency spectrum) that, for orchestrational purposes, places it in the treble, midrange, or bass regions.

PLACING SOUNDS

One of an orchestrator's most important tasks is determining where to place sounds to achieve an appropriate balance within the audio spectrum. Obviously a thicker sound takes more space than a thin sound, so a piece with many notes (fast-running scales, arpeggios, many notes sounding at the same time, etc.) may require timbres with fewer overtones and cleaner attacks.

Use thicker sounds if a piece has ample space between chord notes (theorists call this *open position*), because there's more vertical room for each note. Conversely, a crowd of notes stacked up in a small area of the audio spectrum (a *closed position*) requires thin sounds, or the passage may resemble mud rather than music (see **Fig. 3.4**).

Low notes have multiple strong overtones which often make them thicker than high notes. Except when plucked (pizzicato strings, etc.), low notes also move slower, last longer, and require more vertical clearance than high notes. Consequently, it's much easier to muddy up the low end of the audio spectrum.

Conversely, the higher the note, the thinner the sound. As a result, high notes take up relatively little vertical space. Color, punch, and presence can be evoked safely by doubling tones at the octave, third, fifth, sixth, etc. Also, multiple patches

can be assigned to high notes without as much fear of creating musical pea soup.

FERTILE GROUND

Foreground, middleground, and background comprise the electronic orchestrator's bread-and-butter. They permit differentiation of musical sounds while maintaining clarity, interest, and balance in the overall composition.

These spatial dimensions are well-suited to electronic orchestration because the accessible sounds of one electronic instrument are equivalent to the output of a group of acoustic musicians. Symphonists must tailor the music to the instruments at hand. However, synthesists can tailor instruments to the demands of the music. Therefore, synthesists relegate hard work that traditionally went into arranging to a "pre-orchestration" stage: sound design and editing.

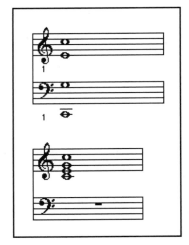

Figure 3.4 The same chord shown in an open position on the top and a closed position on the bottom.

ORCHESTRAL WRITING

*I*f you use orchestral timbres in your music, you should know something about traditional orchestration. Countless books are dedicated to the subject, but here are a few basic facts:

1. The orchestra is divided into four "choirs," each with various instruments: strings, woodwinds, brass, and percussion. The vocal choir can also be added as a fifth category. These choirs offer very effective timbral contrast.

2. Substantial doubling occurs between instruments of the various choirs to form countless timbral combinations.

3. Sometimes musicians are grouped into a "section" (violins I and II, violas, soprano voices, etc.). These groups can be subdivided and individual performers soloed or grouped into "chamber combinations" to contrast smaller masses of sound with larger masses.

The synthesist can apply these principles to his or her medium by dividing sounds into timbral "choirs" or "groupings" for the purpose of contrast, doubling and layering sounds for added timbral variety, and "modularizing" or breaking down sounds into simpler components to form effective contrasts between small and large masses of sound.

A working knowledge of the history of the orchestra helps produce a convincing product. For example, the Oberheim Fat String sound is lush and full but completely out of place when compared to the string sounds produced by an orchestra performing Beethoven. Similarly, the TX81Z brass sounds may be fine for Schubert, but sound tinny and pale with the music of Bruckner. Like most acoustical instruments, each MIDI synth has its strengths and weaknesses. A good orchestrator makes the most of both. —*René Salm and Ron Reaser*

• **The Foreground** The foreground typically consists of a single-line melody, motive, or riff. It also can be defined as anything that stands out in a listener's perception due to contrasts in timbre, pitch, or articulation, or increased amplitude.

Motion moves an element into the foreground. Simply playing a melody in sixteenth or eighth notes while the remaining parts move in quarter notes effectively divides the music into foreground and background (other things being equal). One exception to this rule is a florid accompaniment, where the background material consists of subdued arpeggios or similar patterns.

Articulation refers to phrasing, embellishments, accents, and characteristics of attack and decay such as staccato and legato. An articulated line always receives more attention than an unarticulated one. In small doses, effects like vibrato and pitch bend enhance articulation.

Increasing the relative volume of an instrument obviously pushes it forward, as does adding partials (by opening up a filter, for example). In fact, a brighter sound often seems louder than a sound with fewer partials. Shortening the attack of a sound gives it more bite and generally adds percussiveness.

Another obvious method for bringing elements to the foreground, often overlooked, is soloing. Voice doubling, which can occur at the unison, octave, and/or other intervals, also works. Although pitch shifters create this effect, they are less effective than actual doubling, where timbres, volume levels, panning, and articulation can be individually altered. Other effects, such as chorus, reverb, and tremolo, thicken sounds and aid articulation. A powerful but underused technique called *heterophony* (see sidebar, "Heterophony," for more) goes beyond voice doubling and effects.

Finally, all else being equal, a higher-pitched sound maintains the foreground more effectively than a lower-pitched one. This is why the top notes of a chord are heard distinctly, and why melodies usually are placed on top of homophonic textures of melody plus accompaniment.

TEN PRINCIPLES OF ELECTRONIC ORCHESTRATION

- Use the whole acoustic range: treble, midrange, and bass.
- Use the entire amplitude range, from soft to loud.
- Be colorful: Use all the main timbral groups.
- Use a wide variety of controllers to input data.
- Use the principle of foreground, middleground, and background.
- Create variety through contrast: Alternate acoustic regions, amplitude levels, and timbral groups in the foreground, middleground, and background; occasionally solo one acoustic region and/or timbre.
- Be transparent: Never overload any acoustic region (treble, midrange, or bass).
- Be economical: Say what you have to say with the minimum effective means.
- Creatively use the acoustic space surrounding the listener through sound placement, panning, and motion.
- Use effects, but only when musically necessary.

• **The Middleground** Often music consists only of foreground and background material. But when present, the middleground consists of secondary melodic material or motivic fragments that possess horizontal motion but are less obtrusive than foreground material. Examples include contrapuntal melodies, ostinato figures, and motives punctuating foreground material.

The bass line generally falls into the middleground rather than the background because it is generally strong enough to support the harmonies above it.

For maximum clarity and effectiveness, the middleground and foreground should contrast as much as possible. If you use a legato line for foreground material, consider a staccato articulation for the middleground.

• **The Background** The least obtrusive of all sections, the background generally exhibits little horizontal motion but maintains an extended vertical dimension. Consequently, it often includes sustained tones or chordal "filler" and plays an important harmonic role. Devices used to create a foreground (volume, brightness, articulation) generally are subdued when treating the background.

Be careful with the background, because a heavy scoring hand damages the clarity of the overall composition. With bass, one sustained note at a time may work just fine, while the treble may require three or more notes to provide needed emphasis.

Mixing the background notes in two (or all three) registers effectively furnishes a bed for foreground material and virtually guarantees a full sound if clarity is maintained.

CLASSIFYING SOUNDS

Every synthesist should organize their vast collection of sounds for easy access and use (one example of such a classification is General MIDI; see p. 49). Much like attempting to describe timbre, classifying sound is subjective and depends on one's working methods. Nevertheless, a general and useful way to organize sounds is by the qualities of timbre that have been discussed: attack, thickness, instrumental timbre, bright sounds, dark sounds, pitched sounds, and unpitched sounds. Of course, some sounds can be classified in more than one category.

Change useless preset names like Zoot String, Bible Pad, or Schluba. These only confuse the creative process. Drop redundancies (the word "string" is superfluous in a string bank), and use abbreviations that aptly describe a patch (Horn +5th, Fast Ding, etc.). However, complex or multilayered patches often are easier to identify by a colorful "handle," such as Jungle Chirps.

Highly distinctive patches have great novelty appeal but don't necessarily wear well. As a rule of thumb, the more distinct the patch, the less often it should be heard.

Be aware that a sound's complexity diminishes its flexibility. A sample of the Los Angeles Philharmonic playing a fortissimo chord loses definition and character as you move up and down the keyboard. In general, the more complex the patch, the narrower its acoustic range.

Finally, complex sounds push the limits of clarity. It *is* possible to create effective, complex layered patches, but it takes extra care. To insure clarity within a complex sound structure, use the same principles required for good orchestration: Spread tones over the acoustic spectrum, provide each tone sufficient vertical distance, and judiciously mix distinct timbres.

THE FINAL NOTE

These guidelines notwithstanding, orchestration has few hard and fast rules. The principles and concepts offered in this article are only suggestions. In the final analysis, your ear is the judge. No two people orchestrate the same way, and every synthesist eventually should develop his or her own sound. ♪

HETEROPHONY

Though scary-sounding, this term refers to an often-overlooked technique of combining a melody with simultaneous variations (heterophonic means "different-voiced"). Heterophony is a great way to underline a melody and bring it to the foreground. It also provides an alternative to voice doubling or the use of effects like chorusing. As shown in **Fig. 3.5**, the technique involves splitting up a single melody into a number of parts.

Figure 3.5 Heterophonic textures split up melodies into at least two strands. This works best with contrasting timbres.

Heterophony energizes the creative juices, because there's almost no limit to the number of simultaneous variations on a given melody. If done properly, the resulting texture is almost always interesting, musical, and effective. It's also highly colorful and particularly well-suited to the electronic musician because of such diverse possibilities as independent panning of the linked melodic strands and elaborate echo effects. The technique is most effective when the melodic strands have contrasting timbres.

Heterophony should not be confused with *hocketing* or *pointillism*, two other terms for musical textures. Hocketing refers to the distribution of a melodic line among two voices in such a way that when one voice sounds, the other is silent. Hocketing has one melodic line, whereas heterophony always has at least two strands. Pointillism, on the other hand, is a texture where pitches are sounded in various timbres, largely in linear isolation from one another rather than as melodies.

Heterophony can effectively underline a melody and bring it to the foreground. It also manages to combine foreground and middleground elements, requiring only a little background material to create a rich, exciting texture. Use it!
—*René Salm*

4

Digital Audio and Multimedia

Going Tapeless: An Introduction to Hard Disk Recording and Editing

BY CHRIS MEYER AND GARY HALL

What is hard disk recording? Most simply, it is a way to convert music or other sounds into data a computer can understand and store it on a hard disk. The recorded sound can come from a synthesizer or other electronic instrument, or perhaps a microphone recording a violin—even the sound of a rainforest is fair game. Large hard disks are required because storing digital versions of a sound or song takes a phenomenal amount of storage space. For example, a full-length CD contains over 700 megabytes of data!

Here's how hard disk recording works: An analog-to-digital converter (A/D converter) converts the analog audio signal into digital format. It then sends the digital data directly to the hard disk, where it is stored as a sound file. The file then can be edited and manipulated onscreen in ways that would be impossible with traditional analog recordings. To listen to the sound file, the signal is converted back into analog by a digital-to-analog converter (D/A converter or DAC) and played over speakers.

WHY BOTHER?

Let's make something clear up front: There are many occasions where there is little to be gained by recording to hard disk. If you're looking for straightforward, play-into-the-recorder-and-there-you-are recording, then tape has the advantage. It uses a removable, low-cost medium and hundreds of individual recordings can be kept on a shelf, ready to go. In contrast, most hard disks are permanently installed. When you want to change projects, you have to perform a time-consuming transfer to and from disk. Tape provides far more play time per dollar as well.

So why mess with disk-based systems at all? In a word, the reason is *power*: the power to control sound, to splice, dice, bend, fold, spindle, and mutilate beyond recognition, without ever touching the original. The power to slip tracks, and to trigger audio instantly from any point. Disk audio means never having to say you're sorry. From this perspective, these devices are not recording systems at all, but tools for editing and manipulating sound, the most powerful means of handling audio that we have ever seen.

FROM RUST TO RICHES

With tape, analog or digitized audio is sent to the record head, which is actually a fancy electromagnet. Recording tape—a ribbon of cellophane with a rust-like substance carefully painted on one side—is dragged across this head and "remembers" the electromagnetic fluctuations that are applied to it during the process. For playback, this same ribbon is dragged across a head that converts the memorized fluctuations back into voltages that are processed or converted to resemble the original signal. Multiple tracks are synchronized by printing them side-by-side on the tape. Correct playback speed is maintained by dragging the tape over the heads at a carefully controlled rate. To get at a specific piece of audio, the tape must be wound to the correct spot.

Tapeless recording is an entirely different story. (Generally, when we say tapeless recording we mean recording to hard disk, and the terms "tapeless," "random-access," "disk-based" and "hard disk" recording are used interchangeably in this article.) All tapeless systems are digital, so the process starts with A/D converters or direct digital inputs from an external device like a DAT which has already performed the A/D conversion. The trick is then to save this audio data somewhere. Somewhere could be RAM, but that much RAM is expensive. Enter the hard disk.

Disks aren't as steady as tape in the way they absorb data; they tend to take it in gulps. RAM is used as a sort of data bucket in a disk-based system: Digitized audio flows in as though from a hose, and the disk acts like a cup, scooping it back out as fast as it can (see **Fig. 4.1**). Playback is very similar: The disk pours its data into one end of the RAM buffers/buckets. The information is then drained out the other end in a constant, precisely timed flow. This data is then fed to D/A converters or directly to digital data outputs.

Playing back different pieces of audio on a disk-based system is a simple matter, since any location on a disk is as easy to access as any other. Data can be accessed quickly (though not instantaneously) without worrying about rewinding. The biggest single advantage that disk-based systems have over conventional tape is the ability to play back recorded audio in any order, including multiple repetitions, without a gap. In short, they are an editor's heaven.

ON TRACK

With hard disk recording systems, the concept of tracks needs to be modified. A tape

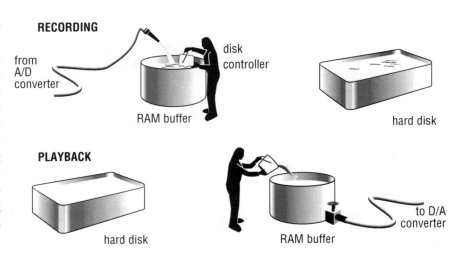

Figure 4.1 A RAM buffer is used to keep data flowing steadily to or from the hard disk.

track refers to a fixed-length holding space for storing audio information. With hard disk-based systems, "tracks" usually refers to the maximum number of sounds that can occur at any one time. What actually exists on the disk are bits and pieces of audio, not necessarily contiguous, that can be patched and pasted together to make up what we ordinarily think of as an audio track. On some systems, two channels of audio are interleaved, or stored together, as a stereo pair within a single disk file.

Data-transfer rates and access times dictate the number of "tracks" that can be obtained from a single disk. In earlier systems, the upper limit was four tracks, but current systems continue to augment that number. However, editing capabilities (the very reason for recording on disk to begin with) deteriorate when a disk is stretched to near its limits. Some designs limit the number of tracks visible to the user in order to maintain true non-destructive, random-access capability.

INPUTS AND OUTPUTS

A system can have numerous tracks available, but if there are only two audio inputs, that's all you will be able to record at one time. Likewise, if you have fewer outputs than you have tracks, you had better be sure that the system's internal mixing and processing functions are adequate for your needs.

Converter quality varies from system to system. Not all 16-bit A/D converters and D/A converters are created equal, and it's worth doing some comparative and critical listening. Nearly all these systems have, or claim to have, "CD-quality" converters, meaning low noise and wide frequency response. It takes practice to tune in to the audible differences. Try feeding audio at low input levels (such as 70 dB down from clipping) while listening to the outputs at high gain. (Don't forget to turn your system down again afterwards!) You may be surprised at some of the burps and chirps that come out. Try high-frequency and low-frequency tones at various levels as well.

STORAGE

Audio recording is a memory hog, and the greatest beneficiaries of hard disk recording may be the companies that make hard disks. Memory requirements can be calculated by multiplying sampling rate (usually 44.1 or 48 kHz) by recording time in seconds. Multiply that figure by the number of bytes required per word, and double the result for stereo. One minute of stereo audio at the compact-disc rate of 44.1 equals:

44,100 x 60 (seconds) x 2 (bytes) x 2 (channels)

or

10.6 million bytes

Rounded down, that's ten megabytes per minute, or over 700 MB for a full-length (72-minute) CD. Disk capacity is a major cost item for a large system. In many cases, however, it's reasonable to operate with much less storage capacity. Also note that data compression techniques can ease storage requirements. However, at least today, it's hard to find a compression system that does not also alter the data (and therefore, sound quality) in some way.

EDITING FUNCTIONS

The *raison d'etre* of tapeless recording is editing, but systems are not necessarily equal in the editing capabilities they provide. When you're shopping around, try to arrange to spend time with the systems before you buy.

Many systems display audio waveforms graphically at any scale, from a complete overview down to individual samples. This is a powerful way to operate with sound, and many engineers have discovered that with practice they can identify individual sound features visually, which speeds up editing tremendously.

But there is a cost. Graphic waveform displays take time to draw on the computer, and large amounts of time may also be needed just to compute the visual display. When zooming, sliding, and jumping

around in a sound file, redraw time can become an obstacle to getting the job done. Pay attention to how long it takes to redraw the screen when you change views. Systems that use limited (or no) graphics to represent sound convey less information visually, but may scroll and move more smoothly.

Two types of editing are possible on a disk-based recording system. *Destructive editing* is performed by changing the data in a file. It may take quite a bit of time, depending on the length of the file and the complexity of the edit. Because all of the complicated aspects of editing are performed in non-real time, and the end result is a seamless piece of audio that does not require any special gymnastics on the part of the playback system, virtually any kind of edit can be performed. The biggest disadvantage is the inability to undo edits or try different variations.

Non-destructive editing is actually performed during playback. A list of start and stop points is used to tell the disk system where to play from next, and all edits can be changed freely at any time. This type of edit puts serious demands on the system during playback, and some designs have problems with complex edit lists.

Many systems use a mix of destructive and non-destructive editing (though they may not use these terms). Often, operations such as delete or cut-and-paste are performed in a destructive manner, while a cue-sheet or playlist representation is used for non-destructive editing. With the different styles of presentation onscreen, the distinction between the two types is easier for the user to deal with.

A third editing option is to create a new file while keeping the original intact. This retains flexibility, but chews up disk space like crazy.

When two pieces of digital audio are butted against each other, the discontinuity can cause a glitch at the splice point. This glitch can be eliminated by fading from one piece of audio to the next. Most disk recording systems provide such *crossfading* as part of their operation. Crossfade edits increase the demands on the system, because two different pieces of audio must be heard during the period of the splice.

Many systems get around this bottleneck by calculating crossfades ahead of time, storing them as snippets of audio that are plugged into the data stream on playback. This reduces the demands on the system during playback, but it means that editing changes will be accompanied by a cycle of crossfade computation. If the crossfades are short—ten milliseconds or so—computation is not a heavy burden. However, if longer crossfades are used, the system may get bogged down. Systems that have speed to spare may compute crossfades on the fly.

Crossfades vary in length and shape. A simple "linear fade" will usually do fine if the crossfade is short, but on longer fades, it may not sound right. A variety of mathematically derived curves are used to achieve smooth edits. Editors also recognize a variety of ways to place the beginning and end of a splice so as to catch the in or out point as desired. Picture a splice at a big percussion hit: If the hit falls at the middle of a crossfade, the attack will be muddied. In this case, what's needed is a crossfade that is completed just at the point of the percussion attack.

SIGNAL PROCESSING

Tape-based recorders have very little signal processing capability, but tapeless systems tend to be fancier. Some units come loaded with DSP capability; they can perform level

COMBINING MIDI AND DIGITAL AUDIO

Whether you call it a marriage, a collaboration, or just a meeting of the minds, the integration of MIDI and digital audio is one of the hottest topics in the music industry today. MIDI musicians recognized long ago that certain types of musical expression—saxophone solos, acoustic guitar vamps, and vocal lines, to choose a few examples—are difficult, if not impossible, to achieve with MIDI instruments. Many computer musicians address this issue by incorporating analog audio into MIDI-based projects, putting up with the problems of synching their sequencers to a conventional external tape recorder. However, as more software appears that brings MIDI and hard disk recording together on a single computer, an enormous realm of creative possibilities is opening up.

There are numerous practical advantages to putting MIDI sequencing and digital-audio recording under the control of a single program. MIDI composers are used to cutting and pasting musical events as easily as paragraphs in a word processor. Extending that metaphor to blocks of digital audio is a major boon, especially when the software doesn't actually change the data but simply manipulates "pointers" that serve as indexes to the data. That way, the operation is fast (only minuscule amounts of data are being dealt with) and the audio files are not modified, so that later they can be accessed in their original form. It also means that audio events can be used many times in the context of a single composition or many compositions without taking up extra storage space. Given the megabyte-hungry nature of digital audio, this is a significant consideration.

This sequencer-like capability allows audio tracks to be broken up into individual phrases (again non-destructively, using pointers) and moved around or replicated independently of each other. This can even be performed on individual notes, providing the ability to quantize audio events. For example, rhythm or effects tracks recorded out of time can be broken down into individual "hits" and each hit locked to the beats of a sequence. Files also can be processed and mixed non-destructively in the same way that MIDI tracks can be faded, panned, or processed, using Velocity and controller commands within the sequenced data.

Perhaps the most important advantage of the combination is conceptual. Integrated programs display audio and MIDI tracks simultaneously onscreen, giving the composer or sound designer instant visual feedback on the structure of a piece, either as an overview or at the microscopic editing level. Instead of being separate entities that happen to be synchronized, the audio and MIDI data can be seen as a single compositional entity, giving the composer a vastly improved platform for creativity.

Consider the applications in rap music, with its reliance on samples, and dance music, which requires multiple remixes and reorganization of both electronic and acoustic material. With conventional pop and rock, MIDI-digital audio integration helps provide seamless fusion of different elements. For video and film production, dialog, effects, and music must be coordinated and mixed. Computer-based multimedia production ties sound (including music) to graphics, which are either created on an external medium or generated by the same computer. In these and other non-musical events, the MIDI-digital audio connection can be used to great advantage.

As the barrier between MIDI and digital audio comes down, hardware and software platforms are being developed to integrate the two forms in ways previously undreamed of. By taking advantage of the efficiency of MIDI and the flexibility of digital audio, these new tools open up new dimensions of creative expression for the computer composer. The near future promises to be an exciting time. —*Dennis Miller with Paul D. Lehrman* changes, panning, EQ, and even sample-rate conversion and pitch-shifting on the recorded audio.

It's important at this point to distinguish between real-time and non-real-time processes. Real-time processes are performed during playback, giving the operator the flexibility to change any aspect of processing as desired. Non-real-time processing must be performed by rewriting the data to disk. The time involved (often a multiple of the length of the file) and limited ability to undo make non-real-time functions less attractive to the user than real-time processing.

The advantage of non-real-time processing is that extremely elaborate functions can be performed. A very popular example is time-stretching and time-compression. This is useful, for instance, when working on commercials, when a 31-second music track must fit a 29-second narration. The quality of time-compression algorithms varies drastically, so if time alteration is important for your application, audition before you buy.

BACKING UP

What do you do with your audio data when you've finished one song and want to start another? With tape decks, you simply take off one reel of tape and plop on another. However, backing up a disk-based system involves more than just recording the audio: You also want the backup to retain all the directories and information about edits that existed in the original.

DAT is a potentially cost-effective solution, particularly since it also can be used as the "mixdown" deck for the final product. Some manufacturers now provide the means for transferring not only audio data but also editing information to the digital inputs of a DAT machine. However, an audio DAT deck can be a slow form of backup and may not be as reliable as desired. Data DAT is another story. These tape drives are not designed for audio at all, meaning they generally can't be used as mix-down decks. However, they are fast and reliable and can hold 2 gigabytes of information on a single inexpensive data DAT tape.

Another solution is data-tape backup. Tape drives designed for backing up hard disk systems usually cost well under $1,000 and can handle loads of data (hundreds of megabytes) on a tape cartridge that costs well under $100.

There's also the possibility of backing up or even recording to a removable disk of some sort (see "Storage for Digital Audio" on p. 92).

SHORT-TERM TRENDS

Disk-based recording systems have come a long way in a short time and are becoming established as effective tools for audio and multimedia production. While still not cheap, they have fallen markedly in price, and indications are that further reductions in the cost of a basic system can be expected. At the same time, there are still reasons why higher-priced products will continue to have the edge in speed, tracks, and overall capacity.

If you are selecting a system now, seriously consider your real needs, your potential applications, and your budget. Then arrange to spend time on as many of the candidate systems as you can. Many of the differences between systems are not evident from the sales literature because they involve comparisons of the speed of task performance, and personal preference certainly plays a role. The best way to get the feel of a system and how it can help you in your work is through actual use. ♪

Storage for Digital Audio

BY
DAVID (RUDY)
TRUBITT

Computer musicians are a fortunate lot. We have access to technology that our relatively small market never would have developed on its own; the huge group of general-purpose computer users with needs similar to ours supports the ongoing development of great toys. But every now and then, our requirements diverge from those of the herd. During these moments of vulnerability we must stay alert, lest we get bogged down by computer woes that distract us from working on music.

Mass storage is an excellent example. The computer industry as a whole is begging for larger, faster, and cheaper storage. This is great news, considering how much disk space digital audio uses. Unfortunately, digital audio makes unusual demands on storage media: During recording, the stream of data is unrelenting, and your disk must keep up the pace indefinitely.

TURN UP THE HEAT

"Most mass storage is designed and tested for burst performance," says Mark Doenges of Spectral Synthesis, a PC-based digital-audio developer. "It doesn't get tested to see if it can sustain those burst rates for 30 minutes." Often it can't; heat-related expansion alters the precise tolerances of high-capacity hard-disk mechanisms.

"If the disk material expands or con- tracts due to tilt or thermal difference, you might not be tracking correctly any more," says Verner Glinka of optical-drive manu- facturer MaxOptix. "You need a mecha- nism to compensate for thermal expansion." This mechanism, called thermal calibration, ensures that the drive head stays centered over the ap- propriate track. In turn, this insures data integrity—the top priority for general-pur- pose computer users.

However, an acceptable solution for the masses creates a special problem for us. "Thermal calibration can interrupt read or write access," says Digidesign's Michael Abowd. "If the drive's buffer is not large enough to spool during this adjustment, an audio dropout will occur." This means an audible glitch that could ruin a mix pass, or worse, spoil that perfect vocal take you just recorded.

Therefore, choosing an appropriate drive for hard-disk recording isn't as simple as ordering the biggest one you can afford from the back of a magazine. First, call the company that wrote your digital audio software. They'll probably suggest that you buy a drive from them. Although they typically charge more than a mail-or- der house, it's not an unreasonable re- quest. Hardware-related questions are a major part of these companies' technical support burdens. If they don't sell you the drive but you still need their help to make it work...well, you can see their point. By selling you both software *and* hardware, they are making a promise that the entire system will work together. If you're earning money with your setup, down time will cost you more than the money you saved buying through mail order.

ON THE CHEAP

But what if you have more time than money? The temptation to save a buck is strong, but be careful. Drive models, specifications, and ROM revisions change constantly. "Lists of appropriate drives are hard to keep up-to-date," says Abowd. "We recommend you buy from a reputable retailer who will take a return if it doesn't work. Find a dealer who knows digital audio and can work with you." Another option is a consultant with experience in the field.

If you want to test a drive, try this: Using the highest sampling rate possible, record the maximum number of simultaneous tracks non-stop until the disk is full. Then listen back for any clicks, pops, or other discontinuities. According to Abowd, you also should be prepared to "take the personality from your personal computer" by removing all non-essential desk accessories, TSR programs, extensions, and the like. These software extras take valuable memory and processor attention.

Next, how much disk space do you need? If you plan on sequencing enough material for a full CD, you'll be quite comfortable with a gigabyte (which provides ample space for undos). However, these giga-drives are among the biggest and most expensive hard disks available. Simon Berry of DynaTek, a company specializing in rack-mounted drive assemblies, offers some advice. "I try to configure people with the smallest size that will do the job, as there's always changes in size and availability. I also let them know that they should have 20 percent headroom on the hard drive—when disks are close to being full, they act pretty weird."

STORAGE OPTIONS

Although most people start with a good-sized fixed hard disk, there are a number of other options available for your second unit. If you need to work on many small

projects and/or transport sound data between studios, consider a removable cartridge drive such as the well-known SyQuest 40 or 80 MB removable hard disk. Some SyQuest drives have a reputation for crashing, though, so *caveat emptor.*

Removable drives with larger capacities also are available, including magneto-optical disks (MO). A 5.25-inch MO disk holds 325 MB on each side. The disk is flipped manually for a full 650 MB. There are several different MO formats, however, and not all are compatible. An International Standards Organization (ISO) standard exists for 5.25-inch, 650 MB disks, but ISO compatibility does not guarantee a disk will work with different drives and driver software.

One potential problem is the rotational speed of the disk. Faster rotation means better drive performance, but media and drives with different speeds are not always compatible. Also, some companies do not adhere to the ISO format. For example, MaxOptix's Tahiti II drive can read and write ISO-standard disks, but it also has a more dense format that raises the capacity to about 1 GB. The ISO group is considering double and triple density formats that would raise capacities further, but the details of the revised spec are far from complete.

A new crop of lower-cost 128 and 256 MB, 3.5-inch MO drives is available as well. These drives haven't been thoroughly

Spectral Synthesis Digital Studio (hard-disk recorder). Four high-capacity hard disks are shown at the top of the rack unit on right.

tested with digital audio applications, but initial reports are promising. As with any other type of storage technology, make sure an MO drive is compatible with your software and hardware before you buy.

THE NEED FOR SPEED

The performance of MO drives has historically lagged behind that of conventional hard disks, mostly because writing data to an MO drive requires two or three passes: one to erase what was there before, another to write something new, and an optional third for verification. You can record stereo sound files onto an MO drive, but operations such as normalization that require a great deal of disk access are noticeably slower. The playback performance of MO drives is somewhat closer to hard-disk performance, because only one pass is required to read the data.

MO is very resistant to environmental hazards that threaten conventional media, such as dust, mechanical shock, and stray magnetic fields. "I've only fried one MO in six months," says Sound Tools user Mark Wlodarkiewicz, a freelance film sound editor at the Saul Zantz Co. film center in Berkeley, California. "The room had an incredible amount of static. I was putting the disk in the drive and there was this crackle. *Norton Utilities* brought it back, but I eventually had to reformat it, although I'm still using the same disk."

MO excels as a transport medium, allowing users to work on the same project at several sites. "MO is really going to change the way we work," explains Wlodarkiewicz. "We couldn't have done these types of projects three years ago."

One of the manufacturers trying to address digital audio's demands is Pinnacle Micro. Their PMO-650 5.25-inch MO drive exceeds previous MO performance (see **Fig. 4.2**) by using a fast internal processor, spinning the disk at high speed (3,600 rpm, vs. 2,400 rpm on most drives), offering a 4 MB RAM buffer, and utilizing a lighter split-optics head design. Besides moving faster, this head assembly performs a write-verify during the same rotation as the write. The drive is said to be

Figure 4.2 The Pinnacle Micro PMO-650 magneto-optical drive offers faster performance for digital audio applications than most competing drives.

compatible with lower-rpm media, although performance is reduced.

Sam Ward of Elephant Music has configured MO drives with a variety of samplers, and he points out an advantage for those who have both. "One big hard drive must be formatted for either the sampler or the Mac," says Ward. "When you buy a removable optical drive, you've got the equivalent of all these little partitions that can be in different formats." By sharing the same drive mechanism for your Mac and sampler(s), you also share the cost, making the MO option more attractive.

BUY THE RIGHT DRIVE

Buying the right drive is not easy. There's no substitute for proper research and first-hand advice from those who have gone before you; make some phone calls early in the shopping process. And remember that your options will continue to change. "Things are moving along pretty quickly," says WaveFrame's Gus Skinas. "The usefulness of these systems depends on advancements in storage technology. We're all waiting for better, faster technology, and we're all ready to consider the alternatives that might pop up." ♪

Understanding SCSI

Computers, like electronic musical instruments, tend to expand beyond themselves. Add an external drive for hard-disk recording (or a scanner for desktop publishing) to your base machine and suddenly you have a *system*.

Any system of components requires a common means of connection and communication. MIDI covers that need in the world of electronic music. In the computer world, the Small Computer Systems Interface, or SCSI (usually pronounced "scuzzy"), is commonly used to connect computers with data storage and other peripheral devices.

Although SCSI serves a different purpose than MIDI, there are some similarities between the two. Both are used to transfer digital information between pieces of equipment from different manufacturers. Both systems allow "daisy-chaining" equipment on a single line, and both use a system of numbered "channels" or "IDs" to direct messages to the right pieces of equipment in the chain.

Now for the differences. MIDI is a *serial* interface, transmitting one bit of data at a time, while SCSI transfers entire bytes of information over eight parallel lines. SCSI's transmission rate over each wire is also

higher, so the overall data rate is much higher; the actual performance of SCSI devices varies widely, but the interface itself carries data more than a thousand times faster than MIDI.

MIDI has limited bidirectionality: Only one device can transmit messages on a single cable. As a result, most MIDI messages are short commands, with no provision for a response or acknowledgement from the target device. SCSI, on the other hand, uses a time-shared bus to exchange information in both directions on the same physical cable. SCSI message protocols involve a lot of *handshaking,* in which devices exchange requests and acknowledgements. This is a far more reliable way to transmit large blocks of data. SCSI's message set also is oriented toward transferring and organizing large blocks of information, such as computer programs and data files.

The systems also differ in the way they daisy-chain equipment. At each stage in a chain of MIDI equipment, data is buffered and retransmitted via the MIDI Thru jack. In a SCSI system, each device attaches directly to a common bus. This allows for high-speed bidirectional messaging, but it makes SCSI more susceptible to electrical noise and other forms of interference. SCSI

**BY
DAVID (RUDY)
TRUBITT**

systems must be configured with some attention to termination and cabling if they are to work properly and reliably.

WHAT IT DOES

SCSI primarily is used to connect computers with external mass-storage devices. Samplers also have gotten into the act, using SCSI to store and retrieve large sample files on hard disk or CD-ROM. Most hard-disk recording systems could not exist without SCSI; they need the high transfer rate to record and play multiple tracks of digital audio data.

A SCSI system includes at least one *initiator* and one or more *targets*. An initiator (computer, sampler, or hard-disk recorder) sends requests for information, as well as data to be stored, to the target. In some cases, a single device acts as either initiator or target. For example, many samplers use SCSI to connect with external storage devices. The sampler controls the drive and initiates all data transfers. The same sampler also can be connected with a computer that runs sample-editing software. In this case, the computer runs the show and the sampler acts as a target, responding to the computer's commands.

Although the SCSI spec includes provisions for multiple initiators in a system, most manufacturers (including Apple) have not implemented those parts of the spec. As a result, multi-initiator systems are fraught with problems, including crashes. In theory, a computer and a sampler could share a disk drive; in practice, it rarely works.

A SCSI *host adapter* is required to connect the computer to the SCSI bus. Apple has been a leading proponent of SCSI, and all Macs since the Plus have built-in host adapters. Many host adapters are available for other computers as well.

SCSI connectors take several forms. The SCSI standard specifies a 50-pin connector that resembles the printer end of PC printer cables, and 50-pin rectangular plastic IDC connectors often are used for internal drive connections. On the Mac, however, a 25-pin D connector serves as the host adapter port. A 25-pin connector carries the same information (SCSI only has 18 active signal lines), but it may not provide as much protection against electrical interference.

Digidesign's Pro Tools utilizes SCSI to store digital audio on various media.

Most SCSI target devices carry a switch to select a SCSI ID number (from 1 to 8). In many cases, it doesn't matter which ID number is selected as long as each device in the system has a different number. Some systems, however, look for storage devices at specific addresses, so read the host system's manual when you select the device IDs.

SCSI most commonly is used to connect a single hard disk or other peripheral to a computer or other host. In this case, configuring the system consists of connecting the drive with the (short) cable supplied and (perhaps) selecting an ID number. But things get a little hairy when a system includes multiple devices or when longer cables are needed. In this case, consider immediate *termination*.

PROPER TERMINATION

Imagine that you and a friend are conversing across a long hallway. The echoes from your voices make it hard to understand each other, and the problems increase if you speak faster. Eliminating the echoes (by placing sound-absorbant material at each end of the hall, for instance) restores accurate communication.

In the same way, high-speed electrical signals reflect off of discontinuities in wires and connectors as they pass through. SCSI terminators are little filters that help dampen these echoes, but improper termination can cause mysterious (and intermittent) data errors. "Proper" termination is straightforward in theory, but can be difficult to achieve in practice. Most difficulties arise because of undocumented differences in the characteristics of SCSI devices, cables, and connectors.

According to the spec, a SCSI *bus* (the entire collection of SCSI cables, including those inside the devices themselves) should be terminated at each end. If the total length of the bus is shorter than 18 inches, however, you usually only need to terminate at one end. Long buses (over 10 feet) may need termination in the middle as well as at each end.

When you add up cable lengths, watch for "hidden" cabling. The wiring inside of each device counts. A sampler, for instance, may have several feet of unshielded ribbon cable linking the SCSI connector to the motherboard. Also watch for problems caused by bad or mismatched SCSI cables. At SCSI's high speeds, small differences in cables can cause problems; the juncture between two different makes of cable can act as a reflector for digital signals. For best performance, buy high-quality cables from a single manufacturer.

SCSI terminators come in several types of physical packages. The first is mounted *internally*, right on the drive's printed circuit board. This on-drive termination is a group of resistors mounted together in a package that resembles an IC. These terminators usually are mounted in a socket for easy removal.

Another kind of termination device is designed to mount *externally*, and resembles a plug without a cable. Just slap it onto the "thru" (or daisy-chain) spare SCSI port on the back of the last cabinet, and you're terminated. You should never use an external terminator on a cabinet where an internal terminator is in place.

Note that the Macintosh IIfx contains a slightly different SCSI chip and requires a different external terminator, known as the "black terminator." This termination plug should be used only (and always) with the IIfx.

TROUBLESHOOTING

Most SCSI systems work the first time, even when connected without regard for termination or good cabling practice. If problems do occur, though, don't despair. Think

things through logically, using these troubleshooting tips:

- When powering up your system, turn the host on last.
- Check the SCSI ID numbers of all your devices.
- Recheck termination. Drives can work without proper termination, but there could be "retries" that you don't know about, possibly causing intermittent error messages. Try terminating in just one place at the end of the chain.
- Check for internal termination. If it is present in any device, put that one at the end of the chain without external termination.
- Check all physical cable connections. Bad connections cause strange problems for SCSI, even more so than with audio equipment.
- Try changing the order of devices in the chain, even if one device claims it should be last (unless you can't remove its internal termination).
- Use different cables and/or swap their order. Better still, obtain a good set of matching cables.
- Don't leave cables dangling.
- Don't leave unpowered devices on the bus. If you want to stop using a particular device, shut the entire system down and disconnect it.
- Mac users should use the a program called *SCSI Probe*, a control panel device (CDEV), to help in the debugging process. Similar utility programs are available on other computers and can be invaluable.

Remember that SCSI is not limited to Macs. PC users should note that SCSI on the PC had a reputation for being inefficient a few years ago, but experts agree this is no longer the case.

JUST WHEN YOU THOUGHT IT WAS SAFE

If you plan to work with SCSI devices in conjunction with digital audio, other computer-music applications, or samplers, call the respective vendors before you buy any peripherals to make sure they work together in your system. ♪

The Secrets of Synchronization

While yesterday's home studio was lucky to boast a 4-track recorder, its 1990s counterpart commonly features several recording devices, including multi-track tape, sequencers, and drum machines. This adds power, but also creates a problem: how to make everything work together. Synchronization helps solve this problem, ensuring that everything starts at the same time, at the same point in the music, and then stays in step.

When you record live tracks to tape, you don't worry about sync. Your multitrack is always "synchronized" to itself. It's the only device that has to start when you press play; all the tracks begin simultaneously and never drift in relation to one another.

The situation changes when you bring a sequencer and a multitrack together. Both record and play back music, but they need to do it together, like musicians playing in a band. The problem is that, unaided, your pieces of equipment can't listen to one another. They need a conductor.

Imagine an orchestra in rehearsal. The conductor tells the musicians to begin at a specific bar, or beat within the bar, and signals them to start. Each dip of the conductor's baton indicates a beat of the music. As long as the musicians track the conductor's gestures, they never slip out of time. In synchronization, the conductor is the *master* and the musicians are the *slaves*. The master marks the start and provides the "beat clock," and the slaves follow accordingly.

MIDI SYNC

BY
DAN
PHILLIPS

Your sequencers and drum machines communicate in a similar way. MIDI has a special message, the MIDI Clock, that the master transmits 24 times during every quarter note, like a metronome beating out 64th-note triplets. Like musicians watching a conductor, sequencers and drum machines can get their clock from this pulse. Most sequencers have higher resolutions than 24 pulses per quarter note (ppqn). These devices maintain clock resolution by interpolating between MIDI Clocks.

Many sequencers also use Song Position Pointer, which carries measure and beat information. For example, the master can tell the slaves, "You should now be at beat 3 of measure 74." Song Position Pointers provide a count of sixteenth-note intervals to tell the slave its exact location at any moment. Drum machines and sequencers are programmed in terms of beats and measures, so the combination of MIDI Clocks and Song Position Pointers makes them easy to synchronize (see **Fig. 4.3**). We'll explore other ways to sync up a little later.

Multitrack recorders don't deal directly with conceptual constructs such as measures and beats; they just record sound. To synchronize with tape, you need to relate the recorded audio to bars and beats. This service is provided by an external device, the *tape synchronizer,* that converts clock and location information into an audio signal that can be recorded, or *striped,* onto tape. Once the tape is striped, the tape synchronizer listens to this signal and translates it into the form that sequencers and drum machines use. In this way, every spot on the tape is tied to a particular measure and beat.

To work as a synchronization slave, a piece of equipment must accept control by an external clock. Sequencers and drum machines accomplish this easily, but tape recorders generally do not. For this reason, it's normal to use tape as the sync master so that the more agile sequencers can take on the burden of synchronizing to it.

So far, we've discussed tempo-based synchronization. MIDI Clocks and Song Position Pointers are the computer-oriented side of this type of synchronization, but there are other kinds as well. Frequency Shift Keying (FSK) is a technique for recording tempo information onto tape. Older FSK synchronizers may record the clocks but not the measure/beat location. Every time you want to sync up, you have to start from the beginning. Newer devices, such as J.L. Cooper's PPS-1 and Midiman's Syncman, record Song Position Pointers in the sync tone. This lets you start from any point on the tape.

SMPTE SYNC

Another common type of sync is not related as directly to music. Rather than communicating in terms of beats and measures, it divides time into minutes and seconds. This type of sync includes SMPTE time code and its offspring, MIDI Time Code (MTC). (SMPTE is an acronym for the Society of Motion Picture and Television Engineers.) SMPTE time code originated from the need to synchronize film and its audio components.

SMPTE and its compatriots deal with absolute time instead of tempo. It's the high-tech equivalent of your computer dialing "time" on the phone. In American video, for instance, every thirtieth of a second a SMPTE convertor sends a message like

this: "The time is now two hours, seventeen minutes, three seconds, and eight frames." In response, all the slave units scramble to reach the internal point that matches the master time, like a commando team synchronizing their watches.

While this makes sense, it means your sequencer and other gear have to calculate the bar and beat at, in our example, 2:17:03:08. SMPTE deals only with absolute time and contains no information about tempo or start point. To use time code with music, a synchronizer or sequencer must relate tempo and a start point to absolute time.

Let's return to the orchestra analogy. Suppose you want your orchestra to perform background music for a precisely timed ceremony. You might give the conductor the following instructions:

- Start the slow introduction at 9:05, beginning with a tempo of 100 beats per minute (bpm).

- When the intro ends at 9:07 and 37 seconds, begin the body of the first movement and increase the tempo to 120 bpm.

- At the end of that movement (9:12 and 43 seconds), begin the second movement at a tempo of 87 bpm.

- When you reach the coda, slow down gradually, so that the movement ends at exactly 9:17.

This set of instructions is a *tempo map,* listing start times and tempi in relation to absolute time. For many pieces, the tempo map is just a start time with a single tempo value.

If you have to deal with multiple slaves, you could give each its own copy of the

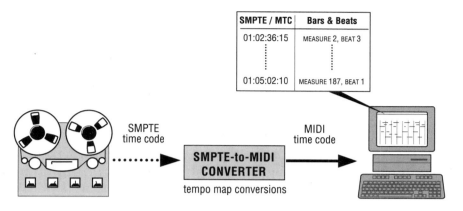

SMPTE / MTC	Bars & Beats
01:02:36:15	MEASURE 2, BEAT 3
01:05:02:10	MEASURE 187, BEAT 1

SMPTE time code ⋯⋯▶ **SMPTE-to-MIDI CONVERTER** ⟶ MIDI time code

tempo map conversions

Figure 4.3 A SMPTE-to-MIDI converter translates SMPTE time code on tape into MIDI Time Code used by the sequencer. The sequencer uses a tempo map to determine the bars and beats location from the absolute time.

tempo map and hope they run accurately enough to stay in sync. A better plan is to let your sequencer or tape synchronizer take charge of the tempo map, feeding MIDI Clocks and Song Position Pointers to the rest of the system. This ensures that each piece of equipment receives exactly the same interpretation of the map.

MIDI Time Code and Mark of the Unicorn's Direct Time Lock are MIDI codes that serve the purpose of SMPTE for sequencers. Unlike SMPTE, they are not recorded on tape, but instead are transmitted between units as a MIDI data stream. Translating between MIDI and SMPTE time codes requires an external SMPTE-to-MIDI converter (see **Fig. 4.3**).

Time code is especially helpful with sound for video. When sequencing sound effects, you can identify the exact SMPTE frame on which the sound should occur and enter it into your sequencer, without having to figure out the measure and beat.

Some sequencers and drum machines cannot use MTC directly. These require an external synchronizer to create the tempo map and convert time code into MIDI Clocks and Song Position Pointers at the correct tempi.

Because time code is a little more complicated to use than clocks and pointers, you may wonder why you'd ever use it, other than with video. There are several reasons to use time code in musical applications, but the most important is that it provides tempo independence. Time code allows you to change tempo after striping the tape and laying down the beginning of the audio tracks; you're not locked into a set tempo. You also can use a sequencer with prerecorded audio tracks: Lay down the SMPTE stripe, then construct a tempo map to fit it. Some devices are able to create tempo maps from someone tapping the keys in time with the music.

In all types of tape synching, start with a sync signal on the tape. Make sure your equipment can read the stripe you record. FSK and SMPTE signals usually go to tape and back without a hitch, but bad levels or a problem with the tape can cause the code to drop out. Occasionally, a reader just refuses to decode a signal recorded on one particular type of machine.

Sync can be a bear when you're getting started. But once you know the principles, you'll keep your studio working like, well, clockwork. ♪

Making Multimedia

U nless you've been locked in a box the last few years, you've heard the term "multimedia" from the mouths of pundits and marketing types. If you're like many folks, you may have wondered what the heck multimedia *is*. What is it good for? What does it mean to musicians?

Ask ten people to describe multimedia, and you'll get as many responses. (To be fair, asking people to define "music" or "computer" yields similar results.) Perhaps it's better to examine what multimedia can be, what some of the components and tools are, and what people are making of it.

Multimedia is the integration of computers, graphics, animation, video, music, speech, text, and live presentation. That was easy. So what's so difficult about defining multimedia? Take any one medium—for example, video—and look at its vast range of applications. When you stir all of these media into an electronic cauldron, the variety of possible combinations becomes endless. In a sense, any application resulting from any combination is fair game for the title.

Just as record albums are recorded in the studio and played back on home systems, multimedia productions are produced using one set of equipment, the *development system,* and performed using another, the *delivery system.* One way of categorizing multimedia is by the delivery system. For example, *computer-controlled presentation* uses conventional slide projectors, tape decks, and video screens under the control of a computer.

Another rapidly growing category integrates media directly in the computer. Such a production might include digital audio, animation, and even video coming off a hard disk or CD-ROM. This is the current hotbed of activity and represents a great challenge to composers and engineers.

Another distinction is between passive and active presentation. Television is passive (despite the remote control), while computer software is interactive. Television and computers represent the most powerful forces shaping our culture in recent decades, and the excitement of multimedia lies in combining them into something approximating interactive TV.

Consumer electronics companies are trying to make interactive television a reality with CD-I, VIS, and CD-ROM players for the home, while big thinkers at the networks, phone companies, and publishing houses are working on ways to pump interactive programming directly into your living room. The big question is not when the technology will arrive, but whether Joe

BY
JEFF BURGER

Consumer wants to be anything more than a couch potato.

At the present time, the two active markets for multimedia are business and education. Businesses constantly make presentations to clients, in the boardroom and at trade shows, and they have an ongoing need for audiovisual support. Slide shows have been a staple of these presentations, but recently the computer has begun to take their place, adding flair (with animation and sound) and random-access capability.

Educators always are in need of new ways to present their material. (You may have thought textbooks boring, but today's generation finds them intolerable compared to computer games and MTV.) Some of today's most effective educational material integrates the look and feel of music videos and arcade games.

Business and education are not separate worlds, either. Businesses must train employees in basic or specialized job skills, and interactive presentations can be more effective (and less costly) than human trainers. Businesses also can educate consumers via multimedia kiosks that use video touchscreens or other interfaces to present information in a user-friendly, interactive fashion. These stand-alone boxes are found in zoos, museums, fairs, malls, and catalog stores.

GRAPHICS

A multimedia production system consists of a computer for central control and various devices for input and output of audio and video. **Fig. 4.4** illustrates this general concept. **Fig. 4.5** shows a typical production system in somewhat greater detail.

Computer graphics often are central to such systems. The images displayed on a computer screen are composed of dots called *pixels*. On a color display, each pixel is actually a trio of red, green, and blue phosphors of differing brilliance. This type of video is called *RGB* (red-green-blue); any color can be represented by the proper mix of these three colors.

A computer's display circuitry includes a video *buffer,* a bank of high-speed RAM that holds a digital representation of the color and brightness values for each pixel. The video buffer represents a certain resolution vertically, horizontally, and in terms

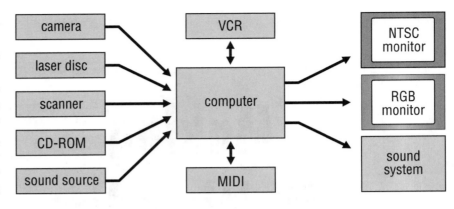

of the number of colors. This collection of data is commonly termed a *bitmap.*

Greater resolution requires more high-speed video RAM—an expensive commodity—and memory limitations often force tradeoffs between physical and color resolution. An average resolution is 640 x 480 pixels. The number of bits available for color determines the number of colors that can be used in an image. A single bit can represent only black or white; eight bits can represent 256 colors, and 24 bits can represent 16.7 million colors.

While 24-bit color is required for true photorealism, the cost is prohibitive for many applications. Multimedia typically uses fewer then 24 bits, but with a *color lookup table* (CLUT) an artist can gain access to a larger range of colors with less burden on storage. The CLUT can be

Figure 4.4 A multimedia production system integrates peripheral input and output devices under the control of a central computer.

Figure 4.5 An example of a typical production system for multimedia. Hardware can be combined in a variety of ways depending on the needs of the project.

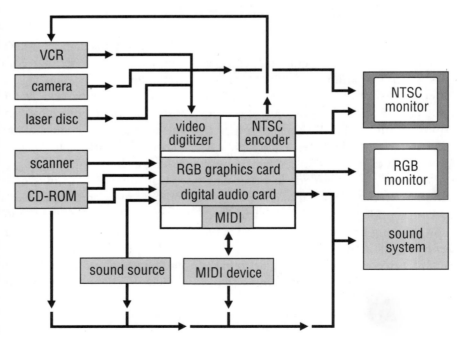

thought of as a number of "paint buckets" that are filled from a much larger number of shades.

Flat, or 2-dimensional, graphics software divides into two classes. *Paint* programs manipulate individual pixels. A circle, for example, is represented as a pattern of bits without identity as a shape. *Structured-drawing* programs maintain a record of individual graphic elements so they can be manipulated easily as distinct objects. Most drawing programs are designed primarily for printed output, so it usually is advisable to focus on bitmapped paint software for onscreen presentations.

Scanners and video digitizers bring real-world images into the computer, converting analog pictures and signals into digital information. Scanners can capture images in a variety of resolutions, with pixel density measured in *dots per inch* (dpi). Printers can use densities of thousands of dpi, but ordinary computer monitors display only 72 to 75 dpi. If you won't be printing the output, there is no need to set the scanner for higher resolution than the display can show, but you should capture as many colors as possible to work with during image processing.

Image-processing software is used to make global changes to an image. If you are going to use a CLUT in the final display, for example, image processing can create the optimum color palette. Image-processing packages also can change the overall brightness, contrast, color balance, scaling, and cropping of an image.

Animation refers to a sequence of images played back fast enough to simulate smooth motion. Most 2-D animation packages extend the paint environment so that you can step through a sequence of images, painting anything you want on each. You also can specify a certain area of the screen (such as a logo) as an object, and the software can move or rotate that object over a number of frames. Some packages can even change one object into another over a series of frames.

All the graphics tools mentioned so far operate in two dimensions. You can scale objects to change the apparent distance from the viewer, but they have no sides or backs. *Three-D modeling* software lets you create objects using wire-frame models.

Complex objects are built by combining simpler models.

These models are arranged and rotated in a 3-dimensional space. They display attributes such as surface texture and color, and simulate the effects of the direction, color, and intensity of light sources. Using these parameters and an angle from which to view the scene, the computer *renders* the final image. This rendering process can take minutes or hours, but it yields stunning effects, including shadows, highlights, reflections, and more.

Three-D animation is responsible for the logo effects you see on TV and the special effects for movies such as *Terminator II*. These applications let you specify motion paths for the objects, lights, and camera over a series of frames. Because a single frame can take hours to render, 3-D animation is seldom created in real time. Each frame is rendered and recorded to sequential frames on a specialized video recorder. Patience is a virtue in 3-D work, since a few seconds of animation may take weeks to produce.

VIDEO

In North America, video is based on the *NTSC* standard to ensure that broadcasts, cameras, and VCRs are 100% mutually compatible. NTSC dictates approximately 30 frames per second, each with 525 lines of 910 pixels. Some of these lines are used for synchronization, yielding image resolution of about 484 x 746.

Video signals cannot be mixed as easily as audio. They first must be synchronized to a common sync source, a process known as *genlocking*. Video decks also exhibit erratic signal timing due to their mechanical transports. For mixing, switching, or editing, the output of video decks must be stabilized using a *time-base corrector* (TBC).

The signals of computer displays and standard video are quite different, and specialized hardware is needed to display computer graphics and animation on an NTSC monitor. Such hardware also can be used to overlay or *key* computer graphics on top of a video source, which is handy for superimposing titles and logos.

A *video capture* board can convert single video frames into computer images.

Video from an external source also can be converted to RGB and displayed in a window on the computer monitor. However, this video-in-a-window does not give the computer access to the video for storage and processing. To do that, you need to digitize the video signal, a more difficult task. Several companies offer video-to-hard disk recording, but the current systems are very expensive and require massive amounts of storage. A number of data-compression techniques designed to digitize and compress video into a more manageable size are in the works.

AUDIO

Multimedia uses the same digital-audio and MIDI technologies described elsewhere in this book (see sidebar, "The Multimedia Musician"). Some computers have low-resolution digital audio built in, and higher-quality digital audio can be achieved with dedicated hardware. Sound also can play directly from CD-ROM. CD-ROM will be described in greater detail later, but for audio purposes it acts like a computer-controlled version of your home CD player.

MIDI is important to multimedia because it offers a solution to the overhead problems of digital audio. CD-quality audio usurps 10 MB per minute of hard disk space and processor throughput. The General MIDI spec (see p. 49) defines standard instrument assignments for multimedia, and sound modules conforming to the spec are now becoming available.

Several manufacturers have released chip sets that other companies are now able to use. Yamaha's FM technology is used on low-end products such as the SoundBlaster, and E-mu's Proteus chips are being incorporated into products such as Digidesign's MacProteus and Turtle Beach's MultiSound.

NEW MEDIA

The file sizes associated with digital media render floppy disks nearly useless, and hard disks are not currently a mass-distribution medium. The present solution for portable mass storage takes the form of optical media (see "Storage for Digital Audio," p. 92).

Laserdiscs contain 30 minutes (up to 54,000 frames) of video per side. For multimedia, laserdiscs usually contain sequences that a computer can access in response to user requests. These images are displayed on a standard NTSC monitor or via video-in-a-window on a computer display. Laserdisc mastering costs from $750 to $2,500, while replication ranges from $10 to $23, depending upon quantity.

CD-ROMs use the same technology as audio CDs to store over 600 MB of digital information. While information can be read from CD-ROM as with a hard drive, the access time is much slower and the disks must be mastered like their audio counterparts. A service bureau can master CD-ROMs for approximately $500 and reproduce them for about $1 apiece in lots of a thousand. CD-ROM drives sell for between $400 and $800.

THE MULTIMEDIA MUSICIAN

To date, music has been something of an orphan in the multimedia mix. As producers strive toward presentations that can compete with Hollywood, however, music is becoming increasingly important. The good news is that music for multimedia represents a dynamic new market for music professionals. The bad news is that the needle-drop phenomenon common to radio, television, and corporate video is sticking its head into multimedia, just as clip art has done in desktop publishing.

Enterprising composers can turn "clip music" into a boon by producing it rather than competing with it. The trend toward MIDI, combined with the realization of General MIDI, will provide a need for musical sequences containing elements to be mixed, matched, and manipulated as needed.

One of the musical challenges in multimedia production is random access. Most people think of audio as a linear concept: music that plays from start to finish. Interactive presentations let the user jump about and navigate through various segments at their own pace. Music must be designed in such a way as to be easily stretched via looping or the addition of complementary passages.

Ideally, the authoring software will let the producer implement fade-ins and fade-outs as users jump from passage to passage. In MIDI applications this would be accomplished via a series of MIDI volume commands; in the case of digital audio, the authoring software must be able to control the playback volume of the digital audio hardware or CD-ROM player.

The other challenge is working within the limitations of the delivery system. If the delivery system includes a CD-ROM drive for audio, mastering your music to CD is the desirable avenue. If digital audio must come from RAM or hard disk, throughput issues may restrict you to low resolution.

Another solution is to digitize only speech and use MIDI for the musical chores. If a single MIDI sound module is used, you must compose for a limited number of voices. If synchronization is an issue, you'll need to learn the ins and outs of *QuickTime* (see p. 115) or *Multimedia Windows* (see p. 113) and "The Secrets of Synchronization" (p. 98).

CD-ROM drives also can function as audio CD players, with the added advantage of computer control. This lets the presentation software access and play appropriate passages based on script flow or user input.

CD-ROM is formatted according to the operating system of the computer to which it is attached. CD-I (or CD-Interactive) establishes a universal format for graphics, video, and sound files. CD-I players are designed as standardized, self-contained units with dedicated user-input devices and standard audio and video output. These machines are designed for home-entertainment and industrial-training applications. Tandy's VIS and Commodore's CD TV are two other (incompatible) consumer standards.

PRODUCTION SOFTWARE

The glue that holds these media elements together is the *presentation* or *authoring* package. The lines of distinction between these two blur, but presentation packages most often are used for audio-visual "slide shows" at corporate meetings. They establish the flow of the presentation in a sort of flip-book metaphor. Some packages incorporate limited tools for creating graphics and other elements.

Authoring software is aimed more toward interactive and/or distributed presentations. Authoring involves programming within the dedicated environment of that software; the nature of programming ranges from pure text to pointing, clicking, and dragging icons depicting functions. Common functions include loading and presenting elements (graphics, animation, titles, sound), specifying transitions (fades, wipes, scrolls), controlling additional media (MIDI ports, digital audio cards, laserdiscs, CD-ROMs), and invoking delays and segment loops. **Fig. 4.6** shows a typical screen from Macromind's *Director,* one of the most popular authoring systems for the Macintosh.

A key element of interactivity is the mechanism for user response—usually a graphic depiction of a button or action that the user selects via mouse, trackball, touchscreen, or function keys. The producer/programmer writes hidden scripts to be executed when the button is selected. Common programming constructs such as if-then-else and gosub/return often come into play here.

Hypertext is a generic term that refers to the idea of referencing different words or passages in a stream of text. If you are navigating through a hypertext encyclopedia, and you look up "music," it starts telling you about the great composers and

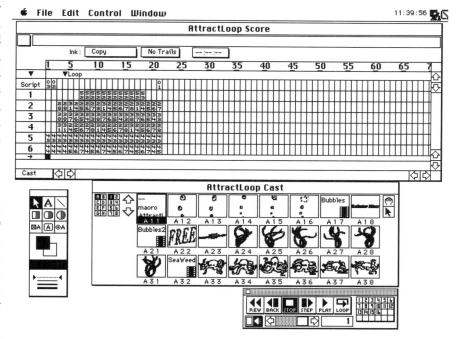

orchestral instruments. Clicking on the name of a composer would take you to a biographical entry (see **Fig. 4.7**); clicking on an instrument name would take you to an entry describing that instrument. *Hypermedia* extends the hypertext concept: Clicking on a composer's "works" might bring up sheet music, and clicking on the image of an instrument might trigger an audio demonstration of its sound.

THE PRODUCER AS JUGGLER

Video production is the process most similar to multimedia: Most full-blown productions in either medium are team efforts. It takes formidable amounts of time to learn the technology and creative aesthetics of each medium, and ambitious productions invariably are on a shorter deadline than is humanly possible. If you want to produce multimedia professionally, expect to work with a team. If you just want to do music and audio, there are multimedia teams that can use your talents.

The multimedia producer excels in creativity, technology, and business management. Producers must be creative enough to deliver a product that is unique and appeal-

Figure 4.6 Macromind's *Director*, a popular authoring system for the Macintosh, uses a "score" metaphor that shows some similarities to sequencer software.

ing, technical enough to know the capabilities and limitations of the equipment, and business-savvy enough to get the gig and finish on time, within budget.

The triad of creativity, technology, and management comes into play in another respect. Making even the best of today's computers compete aesthetically with traditional studio gear is sort of like trying to put wings on a pig. The computer is a powerful tool, but as a delivery vehicle it still has major limitations. Speed, quality, and quantity often are traded off when it comes to audio and video data. The producer must know the limits of the equipment, how to push those limits, and how to work around them.

GETTING THE GIG

The first task is establishing your credibility. This requires researching the prospective client's business and showing them examples of your work. If you don't have a demo reel, create one, preferably with examples close to the needs and mindset of the target industry. Even experienced producers often must develop an example targeted directly at a prospective client's needs. If you are just getting started, do volunteer or spec work to build up your experience and reputation.

Once you establish validity, explore the client's needs, budget, and timetable. The trick is to communicate to a client that quality, speed, and low price are tradeoffs, and they can have any two. Determine how much equipment, if any, will need to be rented. Work out the time requirements, and then factor in at least 25% more. Don't forget to amortize any equipment you own or must purchase for the job. Finally, include the pesky costs of doing business, such as phone bills, rent, travel expenses, etc.

PRE-PRODUCTION

Pre-production may be the most important aspect of any media project; it's the stage where you create the roadmap for the rest of the process. The clearer the map, the easier it will be to implement in production and post-production.

As the budget solidifies, so will the outline and style of the production. What is the client's message? Who will view it and in what environment? What is the client's

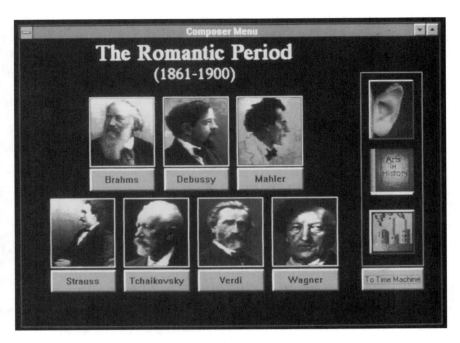

Figure 4.7 In Dr. T's *Composer Quest* educational software for Microsoft *Windows*, clicking on a composer's name takes you to a biographical entry that includes short musical excerpts.

desired image? The answers to these questions should result in a *storyboard*, a flowchart on paper that shows each element to be included. This will normally be a back-and-forth process between your creative vision and the client's outline. Graphics, titling, key frames of animations, and video segments should be roughly sketched. The flow of audio also should be spelled out, along with basic ideas for scripting narrative elements. The storyboard should include a sense of timing or duration. **Fig. 4.8** shows the basic flowchart for an interactive museum installation. The completed storyboard would include more details regarding specific images, text, and audio.

Continuity is key in developing the storyboard and script. Unless the client clearly seeks a new direction, use their existing logos, color schemes, icons, artwork, and style. Remember that music has just as much to do with creating an image as the visual elements. All elements should feel as though they are part of a stylistic family. Employ the same or similar styles for music, the video camera and lighting, graphics, and fonts throughout the piece, and make certain that the styles used in different media components complement each other.

Another aspect of pre-production is objectivity: putting yourself in the viewer's position. If the client wants to identify 25 attributes for Product X, politely suggest that the viewer won't retain more than three. If the voice-over rambles on forever, you'll lose your audience. Think impact, effectiveness, and quality. When everything is agreed upon, get your client to sign off on it in case of later disagreements.

PRODUCTION

Pre-production is planning, but production is actually creating the elements. The most important thing about production is ensuring that the elements will work together. If you want fancy transitions between graphic images, establish a common color palette for all of them. If you can create images or animation with fewer colors, do so: It'll conserve file size and maximize throughput. If music is to fade from one passage to another, watch out for tempo and key compatibility. If animation and music must play back in sync, conduct a test run before polishing up the individual elements.

Throughout the process, organization is important. Label media and disk files intuitively. If others are working on the same project, establish standards for everyone. Keep incremental files as you progress so you can reuse individual elements. Save often, and save well.

In larger projects, production also entails supervising others. The key factor is choosing people for their specific talents; composers, artists, and other creative folks have different fortes. Provide directions that are as specific as possible, and have people submit rough outlines for approval before plowing ahead, but balance this with letting creative people do what they do best.

POST-PRODUCTION

Once the individual elements are produced, they are assembled in *post-production*, using authoring software to establish flow, transition, and timing. Continuity and

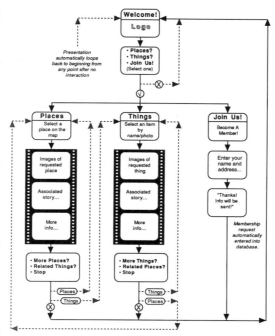

aesthetics are important. Music should fade in and out over uniform periods. Visual transitions should be similar in nature and timing. Establish the duration of each visual element for a smooth flow.

Part of multimedia posting is memory management. One of the things that can throw off a production is waiting for an element to load from a mass-storage device. A deliberate pause can be used to pre-load the next element, and often-accessed elements such as logos or sound effects might be loaded into RAM for the duration of the presentation. (For more ideas on how a complete production is put together, see the sidebar "Project Overview: 'Shoot That Video.'")

FADEOUT

Multimedia is still an industry with its training wheels on. While it has suffered from initial hype and grandiose promises, the tools and market are maturing rapidly. As the field grows, the biggest need will be for new producers who can juggle creativity and technology effectively. ♪

Figure 4.8 The process of pre-production for interactive multimedia includes a flowchart defines all the ways the user can navigate through the finished production. (Reprinted by permission of Creative Technologies.)

PROJECT OVERVIEW: "SHOOT THAT VIDEO"

One of the biggest multimedia challenges is simulating a music video, so here's a quick look at one project that did just that. A client who manufactures PC clones asked us to come up with a trade-show demonstration that would promote their product as a multimedia platform. One of the main marketing messages was that you too can make your own videos for business and pleasure using computers. The obvious solution was to use multimedia to sell itself.

The concept was to create a short music video that depicted someone going through the various steps involved in making a multimedia production (see **Fig. 4.9**) First, I wrote and recorded an up-tempo song, entitled "Shoot That Video," entirely with MIDI gear and the Mac. Next, we set up a video shoot and selected the actor. We videotaped several takes of him going through the motions of using a camera, computer, microphone, keyboard, and VCR in a whirlwind mock production.

During the shoot, two elements proved critical. First, we played back and recorded the music track while videotaping, both as an acting reference and as an audio reference. Second, we used a "blue screen" technique by placing the talent in front of a brightly lit blue backdrop and making certain he wore nothing of the same color.

In post-production we worked with the real-time video limits of the computer rather that fighting it. Using the audio tracks on the video takes as a reference, we digitized one frame of video per beat into the computer, cleaned them up, and made the blue background transparent. The frames corresponding to each successive beat were placed sequentially in an Autodesk *Animator* animation file, yielding a sort of stop-action effect.

A second simple animation consisting of four nearly identical frames looping repeatedly—sort of an animated wallpaper effect—was hand drawn as a background. In a technique similar to audio overdubbing, the animations were merged so that the digitized actor appeared to be performing in front of the new background. The background animation loop was running at twice the speed of the foreground animation, yielding more motion for the same amount of effort. As a final smoothing touch, we told the software to leave faint trails from previous frames when rendering new ones.

Putting it all together, the direct output of the final music mix was recorded as 12-bit digital audio into a MicroKey AudioCard on the PC. A bit of patience in playing around with start times and animation speed yielded an informal sync that kept the frames on the beat. The final result was 7.5 MB of animation and 1 MB of digital audio simultaneously coming off of a single hard drive in real time.

Figure 4.9 A series of screen shots from the completed "Shoot That Video" multimedia project.

Multimedia Sound

Multimedia may well change the way we interact with computers. If it does, part of the reason will be its increased use of sound. While musicians are usually aware of the significant difference that a soundtrack or any sonic element makes, many computer jockeys aren't as well-schooled in the world of audio.

To help you best take advantage of this new realm, this article will run down the key points to consider when taking on a project. Our main focus will be on the most important aspect of multimedia sound: digital audio and hard disk recording.

AUDIO MEDIUM

How is sound used in current multimedia projects? "We're trying to treat our projects like movies," says Mark Seibert, music director at game developer Sierra On-Line. "We use multiple layers of sound—music, sound effects, Foley, ambience, and dialog." Not all developers are creating interactive games, but the sonic elements described by Seibert are common to many projects.

Unfortunately, the low-level sound capabilities of most machines are not up to this task. Speakers mounted inside computers are designed to make warning beeps, not to play music or dialog. Concern for sound quality has increased, but the audio specs of many computer-audio products are lower than they should be. 8-bit audio at a 22 kHz sampling rate and 2-operator FM synthesis has been the norm, although more sophisticated products are available (and more are on the horizon).

But remember, sound is just one medium among the multi. It's not practical or necessary to have CD-quality audio in every application. Even with lower-quality digital audio, sound takes up a lot of space. For this reason, most titles are delivered to end users on CD in one of the several available CD formats (see sidebar, "CD Formats"). Part of your job will be determining an appropriate level of fidelity for the project at hand.

Another major issue is synchronization between your audio and the other elements of the project. With the exception of *QuickTime* (see p. 115), reliable sync currently is a hit-or-miss affair. Although computer audio usually has a fixed playback speed, the attitude toward video typically is "make it go as fast as possible." (In fact, faster screen redraw is a major reason why people buy speedier computers.) Without a single sync source for all parts of the project to follow, the timing is limited by the speed of the user's computer. Programmers can play some tricks without a "master clock," but it's a difficult proposition at best.

BY
DAVID (RUDY)
TRUBITT

FOR EXAMPLE

Before we get into any more details, let's consider a brief case-study for a look at the overall flow of things. *Verbum Interactive* is a Macintosh-based interactive extension of Verbum magazine on a two-disc CD-ROM set. Terry Barnum was part of the team at GTE ImagiTrek in San Diego which was responsible for the Interactive Roundtable portion (essentially the whole second disk). The roundtable presents an interactive panel discussion with six multimedia experts from several fields. To control the roundtable, you click on a question and then simply click on a panelist for their video and audio response.

"All the panelists were shot on Hi-8 video tape and edited on an Avid Media Composer [a Mac-based digital audio/ video editing and assembly system]," says Barnum. "After editing their questions and responses, I dumped their audio bites onto a DAT and transferred it into Sound Tools—the Media Composer did not export *Sound Designer* files at that time. Once inside Sound Tools, I cleaned up their pops, clicks, and lip-smacks.

"Because the Roundtable was produced in the 'Before-Time' [pre-*QuickTime*], there were severe memory restrictions placed on the audio in order to support a frame rate of 5 frames per second. It was determined that 11 kHz would be the panelists' sample rate. So I had to convert the sample rate of almost 200 sound files from 44.1 kHz down to 11 kHz.

"The last step in Sound Tools was to save each file as an AIFF [Audio Interchange File Format] file. Finally, I used Macromind/Paracomp's *SoundEdit* to save the files so they could be read by CoSA's *PACo Producer*, a high-end Mac application in charge of getting everything on the screen and out of the speaker."

The audio tasks break down into three areas: recording, editing, and data formatting/playback preparation. Let's look at these steps in detail with some additional examples from the field.

RECORD, EDIT, FORMAT

First, digital-audio wisdom dictates that you record as hot as possible but don't clip, as digital distortion is a very unpleasant sound. However, this is easier said than done. Chuck Walker, a self-professed

multimedia jack-of-all-trades, knows this only too well. His company, Tree Frog Studios, has provided imagery and sound for a number of companies, notably Apple and Macromind.

"Using the Mac Recorder and *Sound-Edit*, you can play with the input level forever to get the maximum level without clipping," says Walker. "On the other hand, the *AudioMedia* software has a 'normalize' command that searches the whole sound file, finds the maximum amplitude, and raises that point to 100% [all bits on]." However, this technique isn't a replacement for proper record levels. "You're amplifying the noise along with the signal," he

A variety of CD-ROM players

Macromind's Mac Recorder

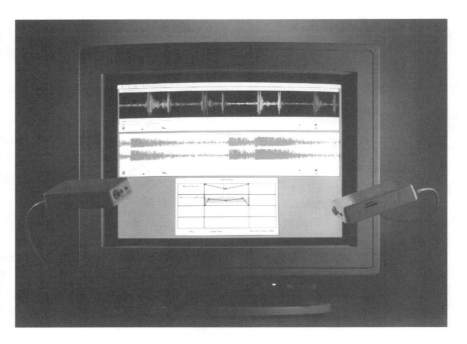

says. But because you're working with 16-bit audio, the noise floor usually is low enough to avoid problems.

You also might try some old-fashioned analog pre-processing, according to Pat Tinney, formerly of Meridian Data, a CD-ROM authoring system developer. "If you're ultimately going to 8-bit, you may want to add a little equalization and compression. When you're removing bits, compression makes it sound a little smoother."

Of course, sample rates and resolution (number of bits) will affect fidelity. However, even if the final product will be relatively low-fi, you still can start with CD-quality specs, equipment permitting. "We hire actors to read the script and record it using Turtle Beach's *SoundStage* and a 56K board [on a PC]," says Sierra's Seibert. "We record everything at 44.1 kHz, 16-bit stereo. We were going to release *King's Quest 5* with CD-quality audio, but with 3000 lines of text, we realized it would take four CDs! Instead, it's released with 8-bit audio at 11 kHz. We also do some stuff at 22 kHz and 5.5 kHz—usually multiples of 44.1."

When reducing the sample rate of digital audio, a steep high-end rolloff reduces the transformation's unwanted artifacts. "We use a Nyquist filter [part of the *SoundStage* software] to stop aliasing when we cut down the sample rates," says Seibert.

After recording and editing, you must get your audio into a data format that can be imported into the overall project. One of the most general formats is an audio version of a Standard MIDI File, the Audio Interchange File Format (AIFF). AIFF is supposed to be supported by all platforms. Spearheaded by Electronic Arts in 1987, AIFF is the collaborative result of many developers.

This format allows the transfer and storage of monaural or multi-channel sampled audio at various sample rates and resolutions. An AIFF file also may include loop points, pitch range, detuning, and other information for samplers, as well as MIDI SysEx messages and data pertaining to digital audio-recording devices. AIFF files usually are used to transfer digital data between applications which don't share a common file format. Also, AIFF is the pre-ferred format for importing audio data to the Philips CD-I authoring system.

PLATFORMS, PLAYBACK

The ability to move sound files between computers is important, since many multimedia titles come in versions for several platforms. One recent project was Macromind's Clip-Media CD-ROM, which includes graphics, music, sound effects, and animation intended for use in custom multimedia presentations. "The Clip-Media CD-ROM comes in Mac and *Windows* versions, which are roughly equivalent," says Chuck Walker, who worked on the project.

"The transfer of the Clip-Media sound files between the PC and Mac proved troublesome," he continues. Although the team had a rewritable optical drive connected to a PC and a Mac, the data was not

CD FORMATS

*M*ultimedia has spawned not only an overabundance of hype, but a variety of new compact disc standards as well. These CD standards are set forth in several colored books. The Red Book, or CD-DA (digital audio), defines the CD you know and love: 16-bit, 44.1 kHz, Pulse Code Modulated (PCM) audio. All other Books are supersets of the Red Book standard.

The Yellow Book is the CD-ROM standard, which adds two new types of tracks to Red Book CDs. CD-ROM Mode 1 adds a computer data track, and CD-ROM Mode 2 adds a track for encoded audio and picture data. An extension to the Yellow Book is CD-ROM/XA, which adds another track of computer data along with encoded audio and picture data.

What makes this different from regular CD-ROM is that CD-ROM/XA interleaves application and picture data with ADPCM (Adaptive Delta Pulse Code Modulation) audio, which uses data compression to reduce its storage requirements. This is important because the program may need to access all three types of data at nearly the same time.

The Green Book defines Compact Disc Interactive, or CD-I. Green Book audio is encoded into ADPCM mono or stereo files and divided into three levels, which indicate the sample rate and resolution. A related format, CD-I Ready, is a standard Red Book disc with added features such as lyrics, discographies, or interviews that can be accessed when used in a CD-I player. The disc may be used in a conventional CD player, but the extra features are unavailable.

The newest CD spec is the Orange Book, which defines writable CDs. CD-MO (Magneto-Optical) discs include a rewritable User area and an optional read-only area that may have data from the Red, Yellow, and Green Book specifications. Unfortunately, the User area cannot be read by conventional CD players. It is also possible to record audio and/or data tracks on a CD-WO (Write Once), but once written, the information can't be changed. —*Terry Barnum* read properly from the disk. Their solution? "We ended up stuffing everything over a serial cable with *Lap-Link*. It took two days. It was like moving the Pacific Ocean with a teaspoon."

Once the data was moved, things went more smoothly. "The Microsoft Multimedia Development Kit comes with conversion utilities for graphics and sounds," says Walker. "It takes any Mac AIFF file and converts it to a .WAV file for *Windows*. It's simple and it works. Out of three or four hundred files, only one got blitzed."

You may need to accommodate a variety of playback hardware as well. On the PC front, there are many different audio cards, not all of which are compatible. Fortunately, *Windows* isolates individual applications from the specifics of the sound hardware by using device drivers that are written only once. Macs and Amigas are more standardized, since they both have built-in digital-audio playback capabilities (although Macs are limited to 8-bit playback without external hardware).

If you're lucky, the final product comes out of a little bookshelf speaker. If not, all your work goes through a tiny internal speaker mounted inside a metal box with a noisy fan. Thankfully, manufacturers are taking greater note of audio's increasing role in multimedia projects. There are people who are actually trying to design computer cases that double as real speaker enclosures. Also, more external sound equipment of higher quality is becoming available. All this means it's a good time to explore the possibilities in multimedia, and maybe even make a little money while you're at it. ♪

Multimedia Windows for the PC

BY DAVID (RUDY) TRUBITT

Ever hear the one about five blind men describing an elephant? Each recounted something different, depending where he was standing. That's pretty much the case with "multimedia computing," a catch-all phrase whose definition depends on who you talk to. Most agree that multimedia integrates music, sound, and graphics, but what you do with this capability depends on your perspective. This article attempts to describe the part of the elephant with the MIDI plug, looking particularly at Microsoft's *Windows* environment for IBM PCs and compatibles.

Windows Multimedia Extensions (called MME), incorporated into *Windows* 3.1, describes standards for using MIDI and digital audio in *Windows* application programs. Microsoft designed MME for use outside the music arena, but if we're lucky, it will lead to more interesting MIDI and digital audio programs on the PC (and, hopefully, drive down the price of related hardware).

One of Microsoft's priorities is to specify minimum hardware for multimedia programs. A Level 1-compatible Multimedia PC (or MPC) must include VGA graphics; 2 MB of RAM; a 3.5-inch, 1.4 MB floppy; a 30 MB hard disk; a CD-ROM drive with audio outputs; a mic input; built-in synthesis; MIDI inputs and outputs; and internal, 8-bit PCM sampling. Practically speaking, the processor powering the system should be an 80386. To help consumers, Microsoft has designed an MPC logo (now the property of the Software Publishers Association) for display on compatible products.

MIDI, MEET MME

Microsoft has fully embraced MIDI and the Standard MIDI File format as part of its strategy. MME includes a simple background sequence player that reads Standard MIDI Files. In addition, MME has the potential to work much like Apple's *MIDI Manager* (see p. 25), but these capabilities are not yet fully developed.

MME receives MIDI messages from application programs (sequencers, patch editors, etc.), and passes these messages to whatever physical interface is present. The reverse is also true—the software passes incoming messages from the hardware interface to the application(s).

The major benefit is device independence: Any MME-compatible interface will work with any MME software (see "Sound Cards and MIDI Interfaces for the IBM PC," p. 22). Multitasking is the other major benefit; MME permits real-time transfer of MIDI data between programs.

MME also addresses the issue of patch mapping, which all electronic musicians face when moving sequences from one hardware environment to another. MME's *mapper* program intercepts Program

Change messages and changes the program number to select appropriate sounds on the connected synth. (The mapper must be aware of the instrument's program list.) Observant readers will remember that General MIDI covers the same ground as far as the organization of patch numbers is concerned. MME's minimum MIDI implementation is similar to but not quite as sophisticated as General MIDI's. Those composing sequences to be played on MME *and* GM platforms will have to confine themselves to the common ground between the two.

DIGITAL AUDIO

The digital-audio portion of the MME spec also should be of interest to musicians. The MME "wave" format includes provisions for 16-bit, 44.1 kHz digital audio, though Level 1 compatibility requires only 8-bit equipment. Several companies offer audio recording and playback hardware, and a group of them have designed plug-in boards that include both a MIDI interface and sound synthesis (see sidebar). With these, customers get everything in one package. Examples include Brown-Wagh Publishing's Sound Blaster Pro and Media Vision's Pro AudioSpectrum. Most of these cards include CD-ROM and joystick interfaces (though not the actual devices), providing a single-card upgrade solution for "multimedia-philes."

The most interesting development so far is Turtle Beach's newly announced MultiSound board, with specs more in line with the requirements of electronic musicians. Its features include 16-bit, 44.1 kHz stereo sampling with 64 times oversampled A/D and D/A converters, and a Motorola 56001 DSP. The card includes an E-mu Proteus chip onboard (with its own MIDI I/O), and also can function as a stand-alone MIDI interface. In addition, the company offers an audio-editing program called *Wave for Windows*. The package includes digital EQ, pitch shift, crossfade, and time expansion/contraction, along with the familiar cut-copy-paste tools for digital audio.

PROS AND CONS

Of course, you don't get something for nothing. While *Windows* and MME offer the advantages of a graphical user interface

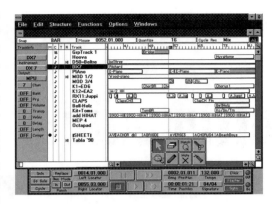

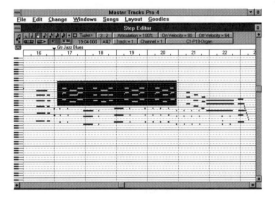

Two *Windows* sequencers, Steinberg-Jones *Cubase* (above) and Passport's *Pro4*.

(pull-down menus, windows, etc.) and the potential for MIDI multitasking, they require considerable effort to get everything running. Problems are harder to sort out when several programs run simultaneously. Also, *Windows* still requires DOS, so you have more to learn overall. Finally, although graphics-oriented software has many advantages, programs using this environment require faster, more expensive computers. Text-only programs such as *Sequencer Plus* or *Cakewalk* (the plain DOS version), run quickly even on older, slower PCs.

On the plus side, *Windows* is gathering momentum in the PC market, and many PC software manufacturers have released *Windows* MIDI software. The device independence offered by MME should go a long way to encourage more development.

Regardless of your choice, there's one development that's bound to boost the marketplace: As multimedia users learn more about MIDI, the demand for music sequences will rise. This could represent new, paying gigs for computer musicians. As far as I'm concerned, that's the best news of all. ♪

QuickTime

As technology marches forward, claims about future developments and applications grow more and more outrageous. Voice-controlled, networked kitchen appliances and computer-generated virtual worlds may appear one day, but I'm not holding my breath. I look forward to another long-sought techno-fantasy, however: movies on my computer.

The computer-video connection is a logical yet enticing development that in many ways parallels early developments in hard-disk audio recording. Early efforts were expensive and somewhat slow in coming, but Apple's *QuickTime* system software has changed that.

QuickTime 1.5 (which may be shared with IBM, following the pact between the two companies) lets any Mac owner view video on a monitor without hardware modifications. This version lacks full-screen, full-motion, 30-frame-per-second quality—you're limited to a 240 × 320-pixel-sized box (¼ of a typical 13-inch color monitor; see **Fig. 4.10**) of 10-20-frame-per-second video with synchronized 8-bit stereo digital audio—but it's an impressive start. With additional hardware and more powerful processors, the software is capable of reproducing a full-screen, full-motion picture with 16-bit stereo digital audio.

Computer movies, it seems, will soon be here.

DOCTOR, WHAT IS IT?

Like Macintosh's internal imaging program *QuickDraw*, *QuickTime* (which works with System 6.0.7 or 7.0) is a piece of system-level software designed to integrate data into the Mac's standard operations. In this case, the data is time-based information, such as video, animation, and audio. It consists of a System Extension—formerly called an INIT, or start-up document—that you pop into your System Folder.

QuickTime's operation basically is transparent to the user. You won't find a *QuickTime* Control Panel to call up features or make adjustments, but its presence adds major functionality to the operating system.

QuickTime's abilities center around the Movie Toolbox, a new set of software routines that let you play back, store, edit, copy, and paste time-dependent data, which Apple defines as "anything that can be stored and retrieved as samples over time."

BY
BOB
O'DONNELL

Practical examples include audio, video, animation, screen-recorded data, and scientific instrument data. The Movie Toolbox and new file formats introduced with *QuickTime* help you cut and paste computer movies between applications the same way you currently work with graphics.

The two new file types defined in the *QuickTime* spec are an expanded PICT format and Movies. The expanded PICT format includes built-in data compression/decompression to reduce storage space for scanned or painted images, and a thumbnail preview for use in standard file dialog boxes.

Movies deal with time-based data and thus comprise the heart of *QuickTime*. They act as containers for the different types of data that the extension can manage (see **Fig. 4.11**). Movies consist of multiple tracks, each containing timing data, sequence data, and pointers to the potentially enormous main data files. (To give you an idea, digital video without compression takes up to 30 MB a *second*. And you thought digital audio had big files!) Movie files essentially are edit lists that tell the Mac when to play certain data files, how long to play them, and at what speed. In many ways, they resemble files created by hard-disk recording systems.

There are three types of *QuickTime*-compatible application programs: those that are simply *QuickTime*-aware (they can play, copy, and paste *QuickTime* Movies), those that let you edit existing Movies, and those that can create and edit Movies. Word processors, databases, and other standard applications could fit into the first category; they'll offer a simple means of playing back Movies within their documents. Existing multimedia applications such as Macromind's *Director* and entirely new applications such as Adobe *Premiere* comprise the bulk of the second and third categories. Digital video editing is a relatively new software genre, and existing programs aren't equipped to deal with the needs of general users.

It's possible that each data format will have a specific program or module written for it and that another program will combine the pieces, probably with the help of System 7's Publish and Subscribe and Apple Events capabilities. Though it's too early to be sure, each of the individual programs may look and function like a MIDI sequencer.

SYNCHRONIZATION AND MIDI

In addition to the glitziness of Movies, *QuickTime* deals with the ugly, unseen world of synchronization. *QuickTime* includes the ability to sync multiple data tracks, including those with digital audio. Each track can have its own timing reference and timing resolution, and *QuickTime* will resolve the differences so that all elements of a Movie remain in sync (see **Fig. 4.12**).

On the surface, this would seem to solve some nasty synchronization problems facing hard-disk recording systems, but in practice that's not the case. *QuickTime* offers timing resolution down to a single sample, but it is not able to maintain pro-level sync because of processor loading from interrupts.

At the moment, *QuickTime* does not include MIDI support. However, according to sources at Apple, future versions will let you add MIDI tracks to your Movies. This would let you create MIDI soundtracks as well as control a Movie's audio mix via MIDI controllers. The preset patch list incorporated into the General MIDI spec undoubtedly will be valuable as Movies become widely distributed.

QuickTime 1.5 can work alongside *MIDI Manager*, but currently no connection exists between the two. Once MIDI support is added to *QuickTime*, however,

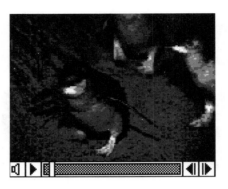

Figure 4.10 *QuickTime 1.5* does not permit full-screen Movies; you are limited to a 240 × 320-pixel box.

Figure 4.11 *QuickTime* Movies consist of multiple synchronized tracks of various data types.

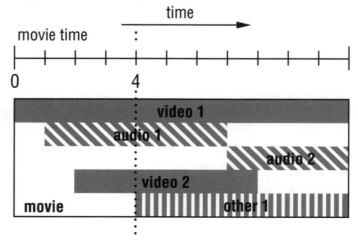

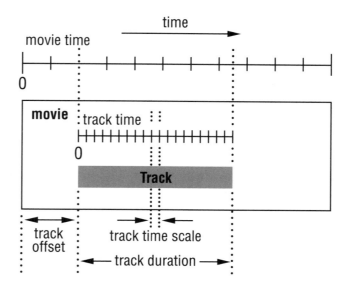

Figure 4.12 Each track in a *QuickTime* movie can have its own time scale. Because *QuickTime* resolves any differences between them, they all remain in sync.

it conceivably could be used to synchronize MIDI and digital audio tracks without any video or animation.

OTHER GOODIES

In addition to the Movie Toolbox, *Quick-Time* includes two other elements crucial to the creation and storage of Movies: the Component Manager and the Image Compression Manager. The Component Manager keeps track of various software and hardware components that would be useful to the creation of Movies, including video controllers for remotely controlling video gear, compression algorithms, and audio- and video-digitizing hardware. The Component Manager is beneficial for the latter because it provides a standardized way for applications to deal with digitizing hardware. In the past, every application that wanted to support audio and video digitizing included special software called a "driver" to support the hardware. The Component Manager removes this requirement by acting as a messenger between applications and hardware. A single generic driver is written for the digitizing product, and as applications are booted, the Component Manager communicates to them which components are installed and which functions they offer.

The Image Compression Manager helps handle enormous files by offering system-level compression and decompression for still images, animation, and video. Apple has developed proprietary algorithms for video and animation compression and uses its own implementation of the industry-standard Joint Photographic Experts Group (JPEG) algorithm for still pictures. These compression algorithms don't adequately replace commercial compression utilities; they only work on the types of files mentioned. However, developers of compression software undoubtedly will create additional compression algorithms to deal with other data types including, hopefully, digital audio. As mentioned, the Component Manager will make the resources of these compression algorithms available system-wide.

CONCLUSION

If you're interested in video-making on the computer, *QuickTime* is a dream come true. It offers a tremendous set of capabilities, and the fact that it will be part of the Mac's operating system ensures that it will be widely used. Actually producing Movies is a difficult, expensive process initially, but the rewards of a home Movie studio could be well-worth the effort and expense. ♪

Appendix 1:
Getting Software Support

The combination of MIDI with personal computers has brought a new level of power and flexibility to the world of music—but this power exacts a price when something isn't working right. How do you find the source of the problem? If your keyboard isn't responding to your sequencer, is the problem with the keyboard, the software, the MIDI interface, the MIDI patch bay, the cable, the computer, the operator, or the system configuration?

Sometimes it's hard to remember that MIDI software is still a relatively new technology. For the most part, the current generation of products work well, but most electronic musicians combine a variety of gear from different manufacturers, and there may be subtle differences between the way these devices implement MIDI. As a result, sometimes the MIDI system doesn't work (or doesn't *appear* to work).

Several software manufacturers offer telephone support in the form of "help lines" you can call for assistance. However, this system works best if calls can be processed efficiently and rapidly, thus accommodating the greatest number of people. Time is often lost because the caller is not prepared with data the service people need to diagnose a problem, or hasn't done any preliminary investigation of the problem. It's best to troubleshoot before you call, and when you do call, to have vital pieces of information handy.

PREREQUISITE KNOWLEDGE
Customer support is not there to teach MIDI basics or how to use a specific computer system. You need to know how to perform fundamental operating system

tasks such as formatting disks, opening and copying files, moving within the file "path," and so on. Users of window-based systems should know how to open and close windows, resize them, and the like. The manual for your computer should contain information regarding these operations, or you can use a number of "third party" supplemental books.

You also should know how to set up your gear's MIDI parameters, such as the transmit/receive channel, MIDI mode (poly, omni, mono), program change and controller disable/enable, pitch bend range, and other commonly used functions. By checking over these aspects of your MIDI system, you often can pinpoint the problem. Remember, customer support people cannot possibly know the characteristics of every MIDI device on the market. If the problem lies with your inability to configure a keyboard for your particular needs, the person at the other end of the line may not be of much help.

If you didn't set up your computer or MIDI system, have the person who configured it write out the entire system on paper; you can refer to this diagram during your call.

BASIC TROUBLESHOOTING
Troubleshooting problems before you call not only saves phone charges, but will teach you a lot. This acquired knowledge could make you a hero someday in the studio or onstage when the customer service folks have gone home for the day. Here are the basic principles of troubleshooting:

BY
JON MEDEK

- **Think logically** Try to isolate the problem, recreating what you did before the problem happened. Don't try to fix the problem randomly; think of the possible parameters involved. For example, if the synthesizer is going out of tune, the problem is more likely to be related to pitch bend than, say, MIDI volume.

- **Don't get angry** A dispassionate, logical approach will get you much further than swearing at your gear.

- **Simplify the system** If the problem concerns a particular MIDI device, disconnect all other MIDI devices and test only that one. With a sequencer, connect a master keyboard with just MIDI in and out and see how that works.

Also, strip down your computer system to the basics. Weighing down your operating system with desk accessories, utility programs, menu bar clocks, screen savers, and so on can result in conflicts between programs. Don't assume that different products from different manufacturers will always work together. It's a good idea to make a special disk from which you can boot your computer that contains the bare minimum necessary to get your system running. If the problems disappear, reactivate your accessories one at time until you find the glitch.

- **"When all else fails, read the manual,"** as the old saying goes. Some manuals have an index, so check any reference to your problem area. Many customer service calls could be avoided by simply spending a little more time with the manual. If you run into some obscure problem and find the solution buried in a footnote on page 126, highlight it so you can find it again.

WHO YA GONNA CALL?

If you've exhausted the troubleshooting possibilities on your own, it's time to call customer support. Always have the following information ready before you call for help:

- **The specific program name and version number** The version number is crucial since some versions exist specifically to fix particular bugs.

- **Serial number** This is particularly important with non-copy-protected software in order to establish ownership.

- **The computer you're using and a brief system description** (e.g., monochrome or color monitor, hard disk or floppy, any accelerator boards or other modifications, etc.).

- **MIDI setup** The type of interface you're using, what method of sync you use (e.g., MTC, song position pointer, internal sync), master keyboard, switch boxes or MIDI patch bays, etc.

Think about your attitude. The person at the other end of the line is there to help, so going into a diatribe about software, computers, or MIDI will not do anyone any good. Be courteous and give the person at the other end a chance to work through the problem with you. You may be frustrated, but it's not the fault of the customer service rep. If you have a complaint about the company, call the company president—don't rail at the support folks.

The more you know about your equipment, the easier it will be to find the source of a problem. Get to know people with similar interests, join user's groups, and always send in your warranty card so you can be advised when updates occur. Good luck, and may your system always work at that important session or live gig. If not...well, you know who to call.

(Big thank yous to Aron Nelson at Opcode, Richard Viard at Dr. T's, and Richard Lainhart at Intelligent Music for their contributions to this article.)

Appendix 2:
List of Manufacturers

MIDI SOFTWARE

Twelve Tone Systems
44 Pleasant Ave.
Watertown, MA 02172
   tel. (617) 273-4437 or *(617) 273-4668*
   fax (617) 924-6657

Big Noise Software (Cadenza)
PO Box 23740
Jacksonville, FL 32241
   tel. (904) 730-0754
   fax (same as telephone number*)*

Coda Music Software
1401 E. 79th St.
Bloomington, MN 55425-1126
   tel. (800) 843-2066 or *(612) 854-1288*
   fax (612) 854-4631

Dr. T's Music Software
124 Crescent Rd., Suite 3
Needham, MA 02194
   tel. (617) 455-1454
   fax (617) 455-1460

Mark of The Unicorn
222 Third St.
Cambridge, MA 02142
   tel. (617) 576-2760
   fax (617) 576-3609

Opcode Systems
3950 Fabian Way, Suite 100
Palo Alto, CA 94303
   tel. (415) 856-3333
   fax (415) 856-3332

Passport Designs
100 Stone Pine Road
Half Moon Bay, CA 94019
   tel. (415) 726-0280
   fax (415) 726-2254

Steinberg/Jones
17700 Raymer St., Suite 1003
Northridge, CA 91325
   tel. (818) 993-4091
   fax (818) 701-7452

The Blue Ribbon SoundWorks
1293 Briardale N.E.
Atlanta, GA 30306
   tel. (404) 377-1514
   fax (404) 377-2277

Voyetra
333 5th Ave.
Telham, NY 10803
   tel. (800) 233-9377 or *(914) 738-4500*
   fax (914) 738-6946

MIDI SYNTHESIZERS AND SAMPLERS

Casio
570 Mt. Pleasant Ave.
Dover, NJ 07801
   tel. (201) 361-5400
   fax (201) 361-3819

E-mu
1600 Green Hills Road
Scotts Valley, CA 95066
   tel. (408) 438-1921
   fax (408) 438-8612

Ensoniq
155 Great Valley Pkwy.
Malvern, PA 19355
   tel. (215) 647-3930
   fax (215) 647-8908

Kawai
2055 E. University Dr.
Compton, CA 90220
   tel. (310) 631-1771
   fax (310) 604-6913

Korg
89 Frost St.
Westbury, NY 11590
   tel. (516) 333-9100
   fax (516) 333-9108

Kurzweil/Young Chang
13336 Alondra Blvd.
Cerritos, CA 90701-2205
   tel. (310) 926-3200
   fax (310) 404-0748

Roland Corporation
7200 Dominion Circle
Los Angeles, CA 90040-3647
   tel. (213) 685-5141
   fax (213) 722-0911

Yamaha
6600 Orangethorpe Ave.
Buena Park, CA 90620
   tel. (714) 522-9077
   fax (714) 739-2680

MIDI INTERFACES

Key Electronic Enterprises
7515 Chapel Ave.
Fort Worth, TX 76116
tel. (800) KEE-MIDI ext. 10
or *(817) 560-1912*
fax (817) 560-9745

Mark of the Unicorn
(see *MIDI SOFTWARE*)

MIDIMAN
236 West Mountain St., Suite 108
Pasadena, CA 91103
tel. (800) 969-6434 or *(818) 449-8838*
fax (818) 449-9480

Music Quest
1700 Alma Dr., Suite 260
Plano, TX 75075
tel. (800) 876-1376 or *(214) 881-7408*
fax (214) 422-7094

Opcode Systems
(*see* MIDI SOFTWARE)

Optronics Technologies
1450 Tyler Creek Rd., PO Box 3239
Ashland, OR 97520
tel. (503) 488-5040

Roland Corporation
(see *MIDI SYNTHESIZERS
AND SAMPLERS*)

Voyetra
(see *MIDI SOFTWARE*)

SOUND CARDS AND DIGITAL AUDIO

Ad Lib MultiMedia Inc.
220 Grande-Allee, Suite 850
Quebec, QC, Canada G1R 2J1
tel. (800) 463-2686 or *(418) 529-9676*
fax (418) 529-1159

Advanced Gravis Computer
Technology Ltd.
1790 Midway Lane
Bellingham, WA 98226
tel. (604) 431-5020
fax (604) 431-5155

Cardinal Technologies Inc.
1827 Freedom Rd.
Lancaster, PA 17601
tel. (717) 293-3000
fax (717) 293-3055

Creative Labs
1901 McCarthy Blvd.
Milpitas, CA 95035
tel. (800) 998-LABS or *(408) 428-6600*
fax (408) 428-6611

Digidesign
1360 Willow Rd., Suite 101
Menlo Park, CA 94025
tel. (415) 688-0600
fax (415) 327-0777

Ensoniq
(see *MIDI SYTHESIZERS
AND SAMPLERS*)

Focus Information Services Inc.
4046 Clipper Ct.
Fremont, CA 94538
tel. (800) 925-2378 or *(510) 657-2845*
fax (510) 657-4158

Macromedia
600 Townsend St.
San Francisco, CA 94103
tel. (415) 442-0200
fax (415) 626-9185

Media Vision Inc.
47221 Fremont Blvd.
Fremont, CA 94538
tel. (800) 845-5870 or *(510) 770-8600*
fax (510) 770-9592

Micro Technology Unlimited (MTU)
156 Wind Chime Court
Raleigh, NC 27615
tel. (919) 870-0344
fax (919) 870-7163

Microsoft Corp.
1 Microsoft Way
Redmond, WA 98052-6399
tel. (800) 426-9400 or *(206) 454-2030*
fax (206) 93M-SFAX

Roland Corporation
(see *MIDI SYNTHESIZERS
AND SAMPLERS*)

RTM Inc. (Distributor of Omni Labs)
13177 Ramona Blvd.
Irwindale, CA 91706
tel. (818) 813-2630
fax (818) 813-2638

Spectral Synthesis
19501 144th Ave. N.E., Suite 1000A
Woodinville, WA 98072
tel. (206) 487-2931
fax (206) 487-3431

Turtle Beach Systems
PO Box 5074
York, PA 17405
tel. (717) 843-6916
fax (717) 854-8319

INFORMATION RESOURCES

Mix Bookshelf
6400 Hollis St., Suite 12
Emeryville, CA 94608
tel. (800) 233-9604 or *(510) 653-3307*
fax (510) 653-5142

Appendix 3: Glossary

In the unlikely event you've run across an unfamiliar term in the pages of this book (ahem), here's a list of definitions designed to keep you in the know.

ADSR Acronym for Attack, Decay, Sustain, and Release, the four stages of a standard envelope generator. See *Envelope Generator*.

Aftertouch MIDI message that indicates the amount of pressure applied to a key or keys after the initial depression.

Algorithm A pattern of information or set of instructions. In electronic music, an algorithm can define the specific set of parameter values to create a sound on a synthesizer (as in a DX7 patch), or specific permutations of MIDI data performed by computer software (as in "algorithmic composition").

Amplifier A device or software algorithm that increases the amplitude of the voltage, power, or current of a signal. Most commonly refers to a device that increases the volume of an audio signal. See *ADSR, Envelope Generator*.

Analog An audio signal is an electrical representation of (i.e., is analogous to) a sound waveform. The signal's voltage fluctuates in the same pattern as the speaker cone that reproduces it. Analog synthesizer technology uses electronic components, including oscillators, filters, and amplifiers, to create electrical signals analogous to the audio waveforms they represent. See *Oscillator, Filter, Amplifier*.

Byte A piece of digital information. Much as each word is a piece of an English sentence, a series of bytes typically makes up

each digital message. In MIDI, bytes are made up of eight bits, and most messages are two or three bytes in length. What's half a byte called? A nibble, of course.

Chase-lock The process of relocating to another device's position in time, then maintaining exact lock-step synchronization.

Chasing The process that occurs when one device (usually a tape machine or sequencer) changes its location to match that of another device.

Click Track Audio "clicks" recorded on one track of a multitrack tape recorder. The clicks indicate the tempo of the music on the tape. These clicks help musicians play with the recorded music, or they can be translated into MIDI sync. See *Synchronization*.

Continuous Controllers A set of MIDI messages, such as Modulation Wheel and Volume, that represent dynamic or continuously changing aspects of a performance. These are the primary means of communicating musical expression with MIDI.

Control Voltage An electrical signal used to control the values of parameters in analog circuits. By sending a specific (or continuously varying) electrical voltage to an element of the synthesizer, such as a filter, you can describe what you want it to do (such as raise or lower the cutoff frequency).

Cue A section of music or sound effects used in a film or video. A cue can range from a short piece of background music to a complex score. The specific points at which the cues are triggered in order to

BY LACHLAN WESTFALL

correspond to visual events are called cue points or "hit" points.

Cutoff Frequency The point at which a filter no longer allows frequencies and overtones of a sound to pass. In a lowpass filter, a high cutoff frequency allows most of a sound through and generally produces a bright sound, while a low cutoff frequency blocks most of the sound and produces a muted or plain sound.

DAT Acronym for Digital Audio Tape, a medium for storage of digital audio on small cassette-like tapes.

dB Abbreviation for decibel, a logarithmic expression of a ratio comparing two quantities, such as how much louder one sound is than another, or how much more power is available at the output of an amplifier than at the input. Also used to indicate the amplitude of a signal.

Digital In essence, having to do with numbers rather than actual shapes or sounds. In electronic music, digital information may describe the waveform of a sound or the nuances of a performance as a series of numbers. The numbers then are translated back into sound or played as a performance on electronic instruments.

Envelope Generator An electronic circuit or software algorithm that changes parameters over time. A sound's volume envelope will determine the different volume levels of a sound from the point it is first played until it is no longer heard. Similarly, a filter envelope will determine the changing brightness of a sound over time. See *ADSR, Amplifier, Filter.*

EPROM An acronym for Erasable Programmable Read Only Memory. This is a type of computer chip that can be loaded with digital information (perhaps a sample of a sound) and later erased and loaded with new information. Standard EPROMs are erased by exposure to ultraviolet light. A newer version, EEPROM (Electrically Erasable Programmable Read Only Memory), can be erased by an electrical voltage, making the chips much easier to update.

Filter A device that removes, or "filters," certain elements or data from an audio waveform or datastream. In a synthesizer, a lowpass filter allows low frequencies to get through while inhibiting higher frequencies; a highpass filter does just the opposite. A bandpass filter allows the frequencies within a specified range to pass, while a notch filter blocks the frequencies in a specified range (see Cutoff Frequency). A MIDI data filter removes certain types of messages from the MIDI datastream.

FSK Acronym for Frequency Shift Keying. FSK is an audio tone, typically generated by a sequencer, drum machine, or computer MIDI interface, that is recorded on one track of an audio tape for synchronization purposes. The tone alternates between two frequencies, and the rate of alternation indicates the tempo of the reference music. FSK can be used to synchronize MIDI sequencers and drum machines to tape machines. See *Synchronization, Synchronizer.*

Guard track A tape track that is deliberately left blank in order to provide isolation between audio and time code or sync tone.

Hertz (Hz) The measure of the frequency of a vibrating object, such as a guitar string or speaker cone. Equivalent to cycles per second. The human range of frequency perception is about 20 Hz to 20,000 Hz (or 20 kilohertz, abbreviated kHz).

Intelligent FSK A form of sync tone that encodes the MIDI Song Position Pointer in the audio track. See *Song Position Pointer.*

LFO Acronym for Low Frequency Oscillator. A circuit that produces an alternating signal at a frequency typically below the human threshold (1 to 15 Hz). Used to create effects such as vibrato, tremolo, and wah-wah. See *Modulation, Oscillator.*

Master Term used to indicate the controlling instrument in a system. If the MIDI Out of synth A is connected to the MIDI In of synth B, synth A is the "master" and synth B the "slave." See *Slave.*

MIDI Acronym for Musical Instrument Digital Interface. A digital communications protocol developed in the early 1980s that allows electronic musical instruments and computers to communicate with one another. The protocol consists of a set of messages that represent various aspects of a musical performance.

MIDI Channel A logical division separating MIDI messages, which allows multiple instruments to be addressed independently over a single MIDI cable. Most messages are sent on one of sixteen channels. Instruments can be set to respond to specific channels, allowing them to play certain parts and ignore others.

MIDI Clocks Also known as "MIDI Sync." A set of messages that communicate tempo and timing information between instruments in a MIDI system. See *Synchronization*.

MIDI Interface A hardware device that connects to a personal computer and translates MIDI into a format the computer can understand.

MIDI Mode An operational state that determines how an instrument will respond to incoming MIDI messages. In Omni mode, an instrument responds to notes on all channels. In Poly mode, the instrument plays multiple notes simultaneously. In Mono mode, the instrument plays only one note at a time.

MIDI Time Code (MTC) A set of MIDI synchronization messages that correspond to SMPTE time code. MTC allows MIDI software to synchronize more easily with time code recorded on film or video tape. See *SMPTE, Synchronization*.

Millisecond One one-thousandth of a second.

Modulation A term used to describe the process by which one element affects another. For example, a low-frequency oscillator modulating a filter's cutoff frequency makes the sound duller or brighter. An envelope generator modulating an amplifier will cause the sound's volume to change over time. See *Envelope Generator, LFO*.

Multitimbral A term used to describe a MIDI synthesizer or sound module that can respond to multiple MIDI channels simultaneously and thus play many musical parts at one time. One multitimbral instrument, for example, could play piano, strings, brass, and drum parts simultaneously.

Note Off A MIDI message used to instruct a MIDI instrument to stop playing a particular note. For example, a Note Off message is sent when you release a key on a MIDI keyboard.

Note On A MIDI message used to instruct a MIDI instrument to begin playing a particular note. For example, a Note On message is sent when you strike a key on a MIDI keyboard.

Offset The difference in time between two events or series of events. For example, if you record a piece of music that starts at one SMPTE time, and you intend to use it in a film where it should start at a different time, the offset is the difference between those two times.

Oscillator A circuit in a synthesizer that typically generates an alternating, or "oscillating," voltage (analog synths) or series of numbers (digital synths) at a specific frequency. This produces a waveform that can be processed by filters and amplifiers. See *Amplifier, Filter, Waveform*.

Parameter A "variable element," according to Webster. If you've ever programmed a synthesizer, you know there are many different aspects of the sound to be specified, such as waveform, envelope attack, and velocity response. Each of these aspects is one of many parameters that, when combined, make a finished sound or patch. See *Patch, Program*.

Patch A specific set of parameter values on a synthesizer that create a specific sound. The term is derived from early synthesizers that used "patch cords" to connect different elements. See *Parameter, Program*.

PCM Acronym for Pulse Code Modulation, one of the most common techniques by which an acoustic sound or analog signal is converted into digital information. See *Sample*.

PPQN Acronym for Pulses (or Parts) Per Quarter Note. The ppqn of a MIDI sequencer or tape-synchronization device indicates the accuracy or "resolution" with which it can represent a performance or communicate a tempo. MIDI clocks are generated at a rate of 24 ppqn (which corresponds to an accuracy of 32nd-note triplets), but many computer-based sequencers feature rates as high as 480 ppqn. See *Resolution*.

Program One of many terms used to indicate a particular set of parameters on a synthesizer or signal processor. Also known as a "patch." See *Parameter, Patch*.

Program Change MIDI message used to tell an instrument to change to a new program. The Program Change message can specify 128 different programs.

Quantization An operation that aligns notes recorded in a sequencer onto a rhythmically exact timing grid. Quantization allows you to "clean up" the timing of your performance by making sure that all of the notes line up with specific rhythmic divisions, such as quarter notes, eighth notes, sixteenth notes, etc.

RAM Acronym for Random Access Memory, a type of storage medium for microprocessor-based devices such as synths and computers. The most common forms are dynamic and static RAM. Dynamic RAM is temporary memory that holds data only when the device is turned on. Static or battery-backed RAM is semi-permanent memory that holds data as long as it has power, generally from a battery.

Real Time Refers to recording or manipulating something as it occurs. Playing a part "on the fly" is an example of real-time recording; editing or recording a performance note by note is not. The latter is typically called "step-time" recording. See *Sequencer, Step Time*.

Resolution 1) The rhythmic accuracy with which a sequenced performance can be recorded. Resolution is typically measured in pulses per quarter note. A higher resolution will result in a more accurate representation of the performance. See *PPQN*. 2) The number of bits used to represent a sample. A higher sample resolution will result in a more accurate representation of the dynamic range of the sampled sound. See *Sample, Sampler, Sampling Rate*.

ROM Acronym for Read Only Memory. ROM typically is used to store data on a computer chip that can be used but not changed. ROM cards allow you to load new sounds into a synthesizer, but sounds in ROM cannot be overwritten.

Sample A digitally recorded sound. When sampling a sound, the waveform is analyzed and converted into a series of numbers. This digitally represented waveform then can be manipulated in various ways

with a synthesizer or computer. See *Resolution, Sampler, Sampling Rate*.

Sample Dump Standard A set of MIDI System Exclusive (SysEx) messages that allow digital samplers from different manufacturers and computers to exchange sampled sound information. See *System Exclusive*.

Sampler A device that can record a sound digitally and play that sound back from a keyboard, or in response to MIDI messages. See *Resolution, Sample, Sampling Rate*.

Sampling Rate The rate at which an incoming sound wave is "examined" to produce a number representing the instantaneous level of the waveform at that moment. Typical sample rates range from 11 kHz to 48 kHz. Higher sampling rates result in more accurate, and often better-sounding, samples. See *Resolution, Sample, Sampler*.

SCSI Acronym for Small Computer Systems Interface. A computer-interface specification for connecting up to eight devices together to form a system. Typical SCSI devices include hard disks, removable cartridge-storage devices, or optical storage media for digital data. Many samplers have SCSI ports and thus possess the ability to add hard drives for additional storage.

Sequencer A MIDI recorder that stores every element of a musical performance as a series of individually editable events. Sequencers can be hardware- or software-based. Hardware sequencers are stand-alone devices that can record, edit and play back MIDI information. Software sequencers are programs running on personal computers that provide the same functions and often include additional features. See *Real Time, Resolution, Step Time, Synchronization*.

Slave A device that only responds to information received from a controlling device. See *Master*.

SMPTE Acronym for Society of Motion Picture and Television Engineers. It is commonly used to specify SMPTE time code, a method of representing hours, minutes, seconds, and frames on film, video, or audio tape. This timing reference can be used to synchronize music to film or video. See *MIDI Time Code, Synchronization*.

Song Position Pointer A MIDI message used to indicate a specific point in a song, typically to indicate the point from which to start playing. An intelligent tape-synchronization device uses Song Position Pointer (SPP) messages to tell a connected MIDI sequencer where to begin playing in a sequence by reading the sync code recorded on the tape and converting it into the appropriate SPP message. See *Synchronization*.

Step Time Refers to recording or manipulating something one step at a time. An example of step time includes editing or recording a sequence note by note. See *Real Time, Resolution, Sequencer*.

Stripe To record a synchronization signal onto a tape track. See *FSK, SMPTE*.

Synchronization The process of ensuring that multiple devices in a music system, such as tape decks, sequencers, and drum machines, have the same timing and control reference. Typically, this includes starting and stopping at the same time and playing at the same tempo. Various synchronization schemes include click tracks, FSK, MIDI sync, and SMPTE time code. See *Click Track, FSK, MIDI Clock, SMPTE*.

Synchronizer A device that allows you to coordinate the operation of multiple devices, including tape recorders and sequencers, as a single system with a common clock reference. Machine synchronizers allow you to simultaneously run the transport controls of multiple tape recorders, while MIDI synchronizers translate SMPTE or FSK into MIDI Song Position Pointers or MIDI Clocks. See *FSK, MIDI Clock, SMPTE*.

Synthesizer An electronic musical instrument that can generate or "synthesize" complex waveforms (as opposed to a sampler, which records external waveforms). Synthesizers often include keyboards, but keyboardless synthesizers or expanders

also are common. Most post-1983 synthesizers include a MIDI interface. See *Amplifier, Envelope Generator, Expander, Filter, LFO, Modulation*.

System Exclusive (SysEx) A set of MIDI messages with which a device or computer program can send information particular to one specific instrument or family of instruments. System Exclusive, or SysEx, also is used for various complex messages in MIDI, such as Sample Dump Standard and MIDI Show Control. See *Sample Dump Standard*.

Tempo map A list of tempo changes used by the sync box or sequencer to determine the correct Song Position Pointer, as well as the correct tempo.

Track In essence, a place to store information. On a multitrack tape recorder, you typically have 4, 8, or 24 tracks on which to record individual parts. With MIDI, it gets more complex. A track in a MIDI sequencer can hold MIDI data that usually is sent on one specific channel. However, MIDI tracks and channels are not synonymous. One track can hold information on many MIDI channels, and a number of tracks can be set to a single MIDI channel. See *MIDI Channel, Sequencer*.

Velocity An aspect of MIDI note messages that indicates how fast a note is attacked. In the case of a keyboard controller, it measures how fast a key travels down (Velocity) or up (Release Velocity). It is not to be confused with aftertouch, which measures how hard a key is pressed after the note has been played. See *Aftertouch*.

Virtual tracks Parts that are to be played by the sequencer during final mixdown. The term comes from the idea that the sequencer parts can be treated as though they were tracks on tape.

Waveform Sound is made up of repeating pressure waves moving through the air, and a waveform is a description of a single cycle of the sound wave. Waveforms can be created by synthesizers or recorded by samplers.

Index

mixing, *5, 61, 63*
modulation, *14*
modulation wheel, *40, 50, 60*
MPC (Multimedia PC), *51*
MPU-401 MIDI interface, *22, 23, 24, 31*
multimedia, *21, 101, 104*
multiport MIDI interface, *16, 20, 30*
multisampling, *12*
multitasking, *17, 18, 24, 25, 113*
multitimbral, *8, 9, 11, 14, 28, 37, 38, 41, 79*
multitrack tape recorder, *4, 98*
music notation, *4*
music video, *108*

N

non-destructive editing, *89*
notation, *16, 17, 25*
notation program, *4, 17, 55, 58, 67, 72, 75*
Note Off message, *35, 40*
Note On message, *8, 9, 26, 35, 38, 40, 45, 60*
Nyquist filter, *111*

O

OMS (Opcode MIDI System), *27*
operating system, *18*
optical drive, *111*
overdubbing, *38*

P

patch, *9, 28, 47, 61, 79, 113*
patch editor, *25*
Patch Map, *51*
PC, IBM-compatible, *16, 56*
percussion controller, *13*
piano module, *12*
piano-roll editing, *40, 67*
pickups, *11*
pitch bend, *9, 14, 35, 50, 60*
pitch bend range, *118*
playlist, *89*
polyphonic aftertouch, *14*
polyphony, *11, 14, 50, 54*
PostScript, *16, 17, 67, 72, 74, 78*

Program Change, *9, 28, 35, 41, 114, 118*
program number, *50*

Q

quantization, *11, 39, 40, 45, 46, 60, 77*
QuickTime (software), *18, 109, 115*

R

RAM, *102*
real time, *69*
real-time messages, *41*
real-time sequencing, *38*
removable hard disk, *93*
removable media, *19*
resolution, *98, 102*
reverb, *15, 61*
RGB, *102, 104*

S

sample, *46*
sample rate, *89, 111*
sample playback, *12, 20*
sampler, *3, 17, 61, 63, 94, 96, 111*
sampling, *11, 12, 22, 81, 109*
scaling, *28*
score, *17*
SCSI, *95, 96, 97*
SCSI terminator, *96*
sequencer, *8, 9, 17, 25, 28, 38, 45, 46, 55, 60, 62, 70, 76, 90, 98, 99, 100*
sequencing, *3, 14, 16, 17, 35*
serial ports, *3, 18, 25*
signal processing, *15, 90*
SIMMs (Single Inline Memory Modules), *19*
Smart FSK, *42*
SMPTE time code, *23, 24, 31, 43, 99, 100*
SMPTE-to-MIDI converter, *100*
Song Position Pointer, *41, 42, 98, 99, 100, 119*
Sound Blaster (sound card), *22*
sound card, *22, 51*
sound effects, *50*
sound module, *8, 13, 37, 38, 41, 104*
sound system, *15, 37*
speaker, *11, 37*

splice, *90*
split, keyboard, *15, 48*
Standard MIDI File, *4, 50, 51, 53, 55, 58, 70, 76, 113*
step time, *60, 69*
step-time sequencing, *39*
stripe, *99, 100*
Sustain Pedal, *35, 50, 60*
sync, *18, 23, 24, 31, 41, 90, 99, 100, 103, 109, 119*
synchronization, *41, 98, 116*
synthesis, *6, 11, 47*
synthesizer, *3, 8, 11, 20, 49, 59, 79*
System Exclusive (SysEx), *6, 47, 55, 62, 111*

T

tape, *46, 87, 99*
tempo, *38, 39, 55, 99, 100*
tempo map, *99*
thinning, controller, *28*
TIFF files, *78*
timbre, *13, 14, 47, 48, 54, 63, 80, 81, 84*
time compression, *91*
time stretching, *91*
track, *4, 8, 55, 77, 88, 116*
transcription, *4, 76*
transfer rate, data, *88*
transposition, *36*
TrueType (type system), *70, 74*

V

VCR, *108*
velocity, *50, 61*
velocity sensitivity, *14*
video, *21, 103*
videotape, *21*
virtual instrument, *14*

W

waveform, *11, 18, 89*
wind controller, *13, 36, 63, 79*
Windows, Microsoft (software), *17, 18, 24, 75, 78, 111*
Windows Multimedia Extensions, *113*
workstation, *37*